# EXTREME WEIGHT LOSS HYPNOSIS
## FOR WOMEN

DISCOVER HOW POWERFUL HYPNOTHERAPY IS TO OVERCOME EMOTIONAL EATING, CREATE STRONG AFFIRMATIONS, AND MAINTAIN HEALTHY HABITS

CHARLOTTE KENDALL

© *Copyright 2021 by C. Kendall*
*- All rights reserved.*

*The following Book is reproduced below with the goal of providing information that is as accurate and reliable as possible.*

*Regardless, purchasing this Book can be seen as consent to the fact that both the publisher and the author of this book are in no way experts on the topics discussed within and that any recommendations or suggestions that are made herein are for entertainment purposes only.*

*Professionals should be consulted as needed prior to undertaking any of the action endorsed herein.*

*This declaration is deemed fair and valid by both the American Bar Association and the Committee of Publishers Association and is legally binding throughout the United States.*

*Furthermore, the transmission, duplication, or reproduction of any of the following work including specific information will be considered an illegal act irrespective of if it is done electronically or in print.*

*This extends to creating a secondary or tertiary copy of the work or a recorded copy and is only allowed with the express written consent from the Publisher. All additional right reserved.*

*The information in the following pages is broadly considered a truthful and accurate account of facts and as such, any inattention, use, or misuse of the information in question by the reader will render any resulting actions solely under their purview.*

*There are no scenarios in which the publisher or the original author of this work can be in any fashion deemed liable for any hardship or*

*damages that may befall them after undertaking information described herein.*
*Additionally, the information in the following pages is intended only for informational purposes and should thus be thought of as universal.*

*As befitting its nature, it is presented without assurance regarding its prolonged validity or interim quality.*

*Trademarks that are mentioned are done without written consent and can in no way be considered an endorsement from the trademark holder.*

# TABLE OF CONTENTS

- **INTRODUCTION** ........................................................................................ 7
- **THE HUMAN MIND** .................................................................................. 14
  - Could The Mind Affect The Body's Wellbeing? ........................................ 15
- **WHAT IS HYPNOSIS? WHAT IS SELF-HYPNOSIS?** ............................... 21
  - What is Hypnosis? ..................................................................................... 21
  - What is Self-Hypnosis? ............................................................................. 23
- **TYPES OF HYPNOSIS** .............................................................................. 31
  - Basic Hypnosis Techniques ...................................................................... 31
  - Suggested Hypnosis Induction Techniques ............................................. 32
  - Other suggested Hypnosis Induction Techniques ................................... 35
  - Advanced Hypnosis Techniques .............................................................. 39
- **THE POWER OF GUIDED MEDITATION** ................................................ 41
- **THE POWER OF AFFIRMATION** ............................................................. 48
- **GUIDED MEDITATION FOR WEIGHT LOSS** ......................................... 57
- **MEDITATION FOR HUNGER ATTACK** .................................................. 65
- **TACKLE TOP WEIGHT LOSS LIMITING BELIEF** .................................. 73
  - Rapid Weight Loss Hypnosis for Women ................................................ 74
  - So How Does Weight Loss Hypnosis Work? ........................................... 75
- **HEALTHY RELATIONSHIP TOWARD FOOD** ......................................... 79
  - Ultra-low body weight .............................................................................. 79
  - Enhanced self-image ................................................................................. 79
  - Rapid dramatic weight loss in six weeks. ................................................ 80
- **OVERCOME EMOTIONAL EATING** ....................................................... 87
- **HEALING YOUR BODY** ............................................................................ 94
- **IS WEIGHT LOSS SURGERY POSSIBLE?** ............................................. 100
- **SUCCESSFUL EXPERIENCE WITH HYPNOSIS WEIGHT LOSS STORY** ... 103
  - Step by Step Approach for Beginners ................................................... 106
  - Ayurveda Exercises ................................................................................. 109
- **CONCLUSION** ......................................................................................... 113

# Introduction

It is no secret that people who exercise and eat right can live longer than those who do not. But which exercises are the best? What foods should you be eating more or less of to enjoy a long, healthy life? And what is the best way to ensure you adhere to these practices for many years down the line?

Find out in this book! We cover how important both diet and exercise are for longevity, as well as some specific things you need to keep an eye on if you want your physical health (and mental health) to last. Remember - a few minor changes now can lead to significant results in the future!

There's nothing better than investing in yourself. By now, most of you are well aware that health is of the utmost importance. That being said, it's always good to be reminded of the matter of investing in oneself. This is just as true when it comes to our bodies.

**So, a few key points...**

First, you need to know that exercise is essential for longevity - both physically and mentally. It can cause you to live longer and feel a lot better at the same time. A 2015 study, for example, found that exercise increases life expectancy by 4-10 years.

What's more, a study from the University of South Carolina and the US Department of Agriculture in 2007 showed that people who exercise regularly live longer than those who do not.

This goes for both men and women. Men who engage in moderate activity live seven years longer than those without any kind of physical activity - around 83 versus 68 years old.

On the other hand, women benefit from increased life expectancy by 5-10 years if they exercise moderately - about 74 versus 66.

**Fruits and vegetables are great for you...**

No surprise here: fruits and vegetables are good for you! They contain vitamins and minerals that can help your body function properly. Simultaneously, people who eat plenty of fruits and vegetables tend to be healthier overall and live longer.

That's the reason why the World Health Organization suggests that adults should eat a minimum of 400 grams of fruit and vegetables a day.

If you are on the road to achieving this goal (which you should be! ), make sure you try to include an assortment of different types of fruits and vegetables in your diet - at least five servings from each category a day. You also need to consume three servings from either the meat or dairy groups each day, so try to find something you like from both!

Another great thing about fruits and vegetables is that they provide your body with antioxidants - which help mitigate some free radical damage in your body. This is a bonus for you.

**Fresh Fish, of course!**

Again, no surprise here, but fish, in particular, have been shown to improve cardiovascular health and extend life expectancy. It's not just eating fish that helps you live longer - it's eating it regularly. Scientists discovered that it helps to reduce the risk of diabetes, heart disease, and other nasty diseases by as much as 40%!

However, there are a couple of issues with this one...

First of all: it's not always easy to determine which types of fish are healthy and not. This is because different types can be high in mercury or other toxins.

A few years ago, in a New England Journal of medicine, nine types of fish - which were commonly eaten in the US - were examined. They are all found to contain high levels of toxic chemicals that have been associated with some diseases. However, small amounts of mercury and other toxins are found in many types of fish - so you can't always rely on one test to show whether any particular fish is healthy or not.

Second: the benefits of fish are not known for every type. For instance, it has been found that eating herring can cause heart disease. However, there's no confirmation yet that that's true for all types of herring.

There is one method that does work, in any case. It's called the DASH Diet - short for Dietary Approaches to Stop Hypertension, which is a brilliant name in itself! The DASH diet is quick and to the point: it focuses on low sodium (sodium lowers blood pressure), fruits and vegetables (they're high in potassium), and lean protein.

It was created by researchers from the University of Miami in 1995 and has been proven very helpful in controlling hypertension.

The problem with "DASH" is that it's not very well known... A study from 2005 revealed that only 3% of people who lived below or above a certain threshold had ever heard of it.

*We should all be eating more fish...*

Fruits and vegetables are great, but you need to replace them with plenty of fish and other seafood. This is because getting enough protein is incredibly important for good health. It's just as important as the vitamins and minerals we get from fruits and vegetables.

A study published in the American Journal of Clinical Nutrition states that an increased intake of omega-three fatty acids combined with protein has been found to lower C-reactive protein levels (CRP) in healthy people. CRP is a marker for inflammation that can increase your risk of certain cancers or heart disease (and make you look older).

So go and start eating more fish! But make sure you're not overdoing it...

**Too much tea is bad for you...**

A study involving 1,972 people revealed that drinking tea regularly can be harmful to your health. Although green and black teas are generally very healthy, drinking too much of them will negate these benefits. The researchers conclude that if you drink four or more cups of green tea every day, you'll be at a higher risk of heart failure than those who drink none at all!

The scientists suggest that catechins - a type of antioxidant found in tea - can increase uric acid levels, damaging your kidneys. The source of the damage is unclear, but it's likely to be related to the amount of tea you drink.

Perhaps the most shocking finding was that even 2 cups of black tea a day were found to be linked with an increased risk of death, simply because they contained small amounts of green tea that was replacing them!

All in all, just one cup a day is fine, but if you're drinking more than that, then you're probably messing up your health. If you want an even healthier drink, try regular apple juice - it has no added sugar and is loaded with natural vitamins and antioxidants.

The best type?

You don't have to go out and buy expensive supplements or tablets to boost your levels. Many of the best vitamins and minerals are found in food.
An excellent way to get the most from your food is by juicing! Juicing is helpful because it enables you to extract the vitamins and minerals you need from foods rather than taking a pill. It also cuts down on sugar intake and helps you lose weight and keep your body healthy, as described above.

Here's an example of a tasty juice that will give you everything you need: (The ingredients are shown in order of what's inside this drink - it doesn't matter which order they go in).

Asparagus and cucumber juice are great because they blend the vitamins and minerals of both asparagus and cucumber. For example, asparagus contains vitamin A which is good for your eyesight, teeth, bones, and skin, while cucumbers provide Vitamin C, which helps your immune system.

Tomato, carrot, and beetroot juice - sweet fruits like tomatoes are loaded with vitamins A, B6, and C. For example, a medium-sized tomato (they're usually sold in packs of 6 in supermarkets) provides 120% of your daily recommended intake of these three vitamins in just one serving! They also contain iron which is good for our bodies - especially for women who suffer from anemia.

Coconut water - a trendy beverage made quickly from coconut. Dieticians say you can drink 1000s of pints of this stuff every day without any adverse effects on your health!

Chia seeds are high in fiber, and even better, they're rich in omega six, which is good for our hearts and connective tissues. They also contain many minerals, including calcium, potassium, iron, and magnesium.

Herbal tea - tons of natural herbs mixed with hot water are widely available everywhere. This is one of the most popular drinks worldwide due to its numerous health benefits on the body and mind.

Lemon water - this is an excellent alternative to regular water due to the bright and refreshing taste. Served in a glass with ice cubes, it will cool you down on a hot day.

# The Human Mind

The weight reduction industry is basic information that just an eating routine or a health improvement plan doesn't guarantee enduring weight reduction results. You will perpetually recuperate all weight if you don't accept that you are thin and solid for life in your oblivious brain. This is one territory that is inadequate in most weight decrease programs. There is, nonetheless, an approach to finish this lost connection.
We like to consider our brains and bodies being various elements; however, both are connected more intently than we might suspect.
You will realize this is substantial on the off chance that you have at any point perused of individuals getting minor medical procedures affected by only spellbinding. The more significant part of us is happy to have sedatives under these conditions. However, it shows precisely how solid the psyche can be!

# Could The Mind Affect the Body's Wellbeing?

Indeed, it does - which is why it delivers profits to zero in effectively utilizing the brain's force. We as a whole can think either particular or negative contemplations all day long. If we need to believe adversely, it can significantly affect our true prosperity.

For example, you can be the individual who gets discouraged and anxious significantly quicker. If anything ends up causing you to feel like this, it can influence how your body reacts to the circumstance; nonetheless. You can improve.
If you end up in a line, for instance, and the most part, begin feeling focused at the measure of time you are squandering, change your reasoning. Take some full breaths and consider beneficial things. Likewise, you can utilize the time valuably and productively, perhaps by conversing with the individual close to you.
The contention is that you ought to be idealistic in the present circumstance. You decide to run out of the store. You needed to pause or feel fulfilled because you had a decent talk with somebody.

**Deal with the connection between psyche and body.**

Attempt presently to see what your feelings mean for the actual way you feel.
Stress can impact us from various perspectives. Long-haul pressure does minimal excellent to anybody; on the off chance that you realize that you are inclined to high pressure, attempt to ease it by utilizing your brain's solidarity.

**Start with the mind and follow the rest.**

This is similarly evident when you start another course or dispatch another business with weight reduction. The thought is that you should initially convince your oblivious brain that you need to shed pounds and that you are a lean and adjusted individual.

It would be best to take care of these ideas in your subliminal self so your psyche can manage you to the possible choices that will understand these ideas.

Logical proof recommends that our ability to get criticism is subject to a particular perspective, a sort of altered perspective. This perspective is a takeoff from typical awareness, which fundamentally works under the Beta brainwave.

At the point when it works, the mind produces electrochemical releases. Nonetheless, there are diverse element levels. You are in beta while you work at your "alert" daytime stage - converse with companions, address somebody, read, tackle a compound condition, or compose an article. Beta waves range in recurrence from 15 to 40 cycles each second. This is the typical brainwave recurrence during the day.

When you sit back after science issues have been addressed, you are in an Alpha state.
When you sit on the train, you are in the Alpha state, and you watch the view streaming while your contemplations go on their excursion. It additionally puts you in this state to ask or contemplate.

Alpha cerebrum waves are slower yet more significant. Its recurrence shifts from 9-14 cycles each second. At the point when you are agreeable in this state, you feel quiet and safe. You have muscles and are available to ideas. The couple of moments you spend unwinding before nodding off is the Alpha state.
It's ideal to re-program yourself to the Alpha state. 85% of all clinical issues (counting gorging and weight issues) incorporate uncertain body agony and stress. Getting to Alpha would assist you with upsetting this unsteady pressure and make your eating regimen more gradual. Additionally, when you consider Alpha, you can, without much of a stretch, reinvent yourself.

**Start by setting aside the effort to unwind.**

A reflective, tranquil day is 20-30 minutes in length enough. Assemble a profound breathing schedule that zeros in your psyche on a sentence, sound, or mantra. The meaning of the sound or word isn't just about as basic as it brings out in you. At the point when your body pressure has released, feed your brain with positive pictures.

Envision the ideal weight—zero in on your thin, slender body and shapely legs. Envision for yourself a healthy and dynamic life. Make it a customary practice for your optimal self in this empowering representation until you can genuinely consider yourself lean, solid, and excellent. Next time you want to wolf a chocolate cake, transforming your brain into a thin body and thin legs.

It was tough for me to figure I should return to estimate 4 when I got additional load during menopause. Presently the hormonal movements make it unthinkable for me to be what I was in my twenties." I reviewed then that I utilized a similar contention as I had made during my pregnancy: "Moms should put on weight." We appear to rely upon commonly acknowledged speculations to decide. Do you realize that your body can be cut as you need? You're 99% water and quantum space, and when you see it, the body isn't tossed into stone or tissue.

Moreover, the visual cortex at the rear of the skull makes what you find in your cerebrum from an organization of substance and electric charges. Your visual cortex design differs from the example that another person or I create. You don't see anything out there. On the off chance that you visit, here you make things (your brain).

Presently we are liberated by that physiological truth - and we realize that we can make what we need now, and we can do it in any case if it's not what we need!!!

**How would we be able to respond?**

1. Protein makes a thin weight, giving the body energetic strength by eating low-fat protein (not all that much creature protein joined with fat and calories).
2. We can start an exercise like tennis, skating, strolling.
3. We should cherish solid, nutritious food and eat great food.
4. We should avoid the individuals who are attempting to eradicate our resolve.
We are liable for who we will be. Nothing attaches us to intrigue except for our feeling of requirement!


Reflection is a decent start, yet you can't do it in a line!

A few groups are more romantic than others; however, luckily, you will turn out to be surer when attempting to get things going. A solid method to begin the connection between psyche and body is to practice consistently.
Most importantly, a short stroll in the first part of the day awakens your brain; it cautions you totally and helps your body feel great chemicals. It likewise has excellent actual outcomes and causes you to feel more idealistic as the day advances.

**Preparing the Mind for Positive Output**

Brain science gave us a scope of assets in programming social changes and thought enhancements to improve a person's state of mind or help this individual better face everyday certainties. Different methodologies, like contemplation, spellbinding, and rest programming, perhaps concentrated clinically. Nonetheless, mind activities and tests with mental boosts empower the individuals who need to prepare their brains themselves and give inconspicuous preparation to improve the psyche's force.

The brain has effectively been pre-customized from our past encounters and learning. Our memory energizes work and gives the premise to reference and differentiation to things that are found.
Any work to adjust what is now the main priority, change recently imagined thoughts, and guarantee that the psyche can endure more than it has done in the past requires a clear difference in mentality in an individual. Each individual decides how they decipher what they see and see and what they envision.

It is as yet our acumen that assembles all the information our cerebrum has gone through. Anyway incredible the mind is, one should note that it is still just a human device, and toward the day's end, it is our finished selves that will proceed to create and advance.
It is challenging to program mind insights, especially for skeptics and pragmatists. Rather than a liquid progression of cerebrum capacities, negative contemplations block ideal thoughts put away in our memory banks, giving our psyches a more challenging opportunity to sift through which ecological components are resources for accomplishing our charming state. Likewise, it is critical to keep an uplifting mentality as this will assist us with choosing what we need and which things move.

This ideological perspective is helped all the more effectively by adding each experience equivalent to our greatness or ideal standard. If we have a particular circumstance and can accomplish it with our minds' force, we will have a more substantial likelihood of making similar progress later.

This is all because of the adjusted perspective we currently have due to the past presentation. Without a doubt, the product idea can do a great deal since it clears the brain and makes it simpler to consider the ideal.

We should be in complete control in programming mind arrangements, thoughts, and recollections for execution. We need to understand what we need and how we need it to be done, and we should figure out how to think, dream and imagine it ourselves and our psyches, and we'll know soon that we live it as of now.

# What is Hypnosis? What is Self-Hypnosis?

## What is Hypnosis?

Hypnosis is a powerful, effective way to change your life for the better. It's been used for centuries in ancient cultures around the world and continues to be used today in modern medicine, psychotherapy, and other systems of psychotherapy.

There are many different ways you can do self-hypnosis, including progressive relaxation exercises or guided meditation. These sessions usually last 20-40 minutes and are typically done each day before going to sleep or when you wake up in the morning. This helps ensure that your subconscious mind stays healthy by providing more positive suggestions as it is most receptive at these times. Self-hypnosis is often used by people who have developed life-threatening anxiety, depression, obsessive-compulsive disorder, and trouble getting to sleep at night.
Many people who have practiced hypnosis notice a significant change in their lives, especially those who well-mastered self-

hypnosis. This happens when the subconscious mind becomes programmed with positive self-hypnotic nature and automatically carries them out because they are more comfortable. This ultimately leads to long-term changes in your life that you may not have even envisioned before doing the exercise.

Here is a typical example of how self-hypnosis can work. Let's say you got into a car accident that was your fault, and you suffer from guilt and depression. You've tried to find ways to rid yourself of these feelings, including multiple trips to the doctor, different types of therapy, and medications, but nothing seems to work.

Finally, after more research, you decide you want to try hypnosis to overcome guilt and depression. You start by listening to an audio on how hypnosis can help with these feelings. After doing that for a few days, you decide to burn the file onto a disc (CD/MP3 format) so that you can listen to it while doing other things such as driving. After listening to the positive and soothing suggestions on the disc, you begin to notice that you start feeling better, more positive, and more content.
You later decide to go to an in-person hypnosis session with a certified hypnotherapist or life coach. After one session, you feel great about yourself and are feeling more confident than ever before. You say goodbye to the guilt and depression that once plagued your life and move on with your life free from those obstacles.

Hypnosis is a powerful way to improve your health, happiness, and overall well-being. It really works! And is effective whether you do it yourself through self-hypnosis or have a certified professional help; you will attain the same results in a fraction of the time.

# What is Self-Hypnosis?

Hypnosis is a naturally occurring state of focused concentration where your mind becomes highly responsive to suggestions. When a person is in this state, he feels more open to new ideas even if he consciously disagrees. He has increased suggestibility and an improved ability to concentrate; he also experiences heightened imagination and creativity. It's as if the critical factor that inhibits or blocks suggestive input has been turned down.

Initially, hypnosis was used by doctors and psychologists for therapeutic purposes. Still, it's now being used by people worldwide to manage stress, make lifestyle changes, quit smoking or drinking alcohol, and so much more!

**Are you interested in enhancing your memory?**

Bryan Neale
Neale, Bryan

Memory enhancement is one of the most sought-after benefits of hypnosis. Studies have shown that highly suggestible people can improve their ability to remember events (both past and future) with hypnosis. If you've ever had a friend ask you to remember something for a specific date or time, then you know how powerful the human mind can be when it's open to suggestions. Memory enhancement is yet another reason why more and more people are practicing hypnosis.

It turns out that people have all kinds of questions about hypnosis. And it's only natural to have questions when you're getting ready to begin a new habit or behavior. So let's take a look at some of the most commonly asked questions about self-hypnosis.

**Is Hypnosis Dangerous?**

No! Hypnosis is not dangerous! If you follow the methods and instructions recommended by the certified hypnotherapist who is guiding your sessions. Some people mistakenly believe that hypnosis involves entering a trance that enables your body and mind to become highly susceptible to other peoples' suggestions. This misconception causes many people to fear being put under the hypnotic influence by an evil person with bad intentions. The truth is that most people who undergo hypnosis are highly aware of their surroundings and respond to any outside suggestion with sound judgment.

**Can I Be Hypnotized Without Knowing About It?**

Yes, you can be hypnotized without knowing it. Although a person can be hypnotized without his or her full consent, this doesn't happen very often. In fact, under hypnosis, it becomes more difficult for a person to perform an action that he/she would not normally do in a normal conscious state. So if someone ever suggests that you do something while you're in hypnosis and don't feel comfortable with the idea, you will probably awaken from your session before performing the proposed action. Hypnosis requires complete relaxation of your everyday conscious awareness and is therefore safe and effective when used with the right intentions.

**Will a Person Ever Hurt Me Under Hypnosis?**

The answer to this question is "No." Hypnosis does not require any particular physical contact between the hypnotist and the subject. Therefore, it is unlikely that someone could use hypnosis to harm or hurt you while you're under its influence. The only reason people agree to be hypnotized is that they are interested in making their lives better.

**What Is The Purpose Of Hypnotherapy?**

Hypnotherapy has been around for more than 100 years. Today, it is used by therapists and counselors to help people control their behaviors, overcome anxiety and fears, and much more. It is a safe method that can be used by anyone regardless of age or sex. As long as the person agrees to participate in the session and desires to be helped (which most people do), hypnotherapy can be very effective! If you're looking for alternatives to standard therapy, then hypnosis may be just what you are looking for.

**Can I Use Hypnosis for Self-Hypnosis?**

Yes! Many hypnotherapists practice self-hypnosis regularly to overcome stress or anxiety so that they can relax more quickly when they're with their usual friends. Self-hypnosis can also be used to overcome habit or behavior problems that we may have. You don't need to buy expensive self-hypnosis CDs or tapes to get results—many people successfully use self-hypnosis just by listening to their favorite music, talking with a friend, or watching TV! Once you become comfortable with this technique, you'll enjoy the benefits of increased focus and concentration as well as improved memory and creativity.

**How Can I Help My Friends and Family?**

It's effortless. People naturally want to help others. So when you learn hypnosis and begin practicing it, simply tell your friends and family members about your new skill. They'll be more than eager to get involved with your sessions—they'll want to be part of your growing success story! They may even ask you for advice on a variety of issues.

## How Long Does It Take to Learn Hypnosis?

Learning the basic skills in hypnosis takes only a matter of minutes or hours—depending on how quickly you grasp the concept and begin practicing. But it's essential to take things slowly so that you don't overload your mind with too many suggestions or expectations. Some people get so involved in hypnosis that they end up forgetting why they started. So, I suggest that you keep your sessions short and simple at first.

## Can I Learn Self-Hypnosis?

Yes! Self-hypnosis can be learned quickly, as long as you have the right teacher. You can learn self-hypnosis using a book, tape, or video. You can also find self-hypnosis CDs which are easily found at bookstores across the country. We recommend that you purchase a self-hypnosis CD from someone who has experience with this technique before starting to practice it on your own.

## Is Hypnosis Just Like Sleep?

No, it is not. Even though they're both very different experiences, hypnosis, on the one hand, and sleep, on the other hand, do have some similarities. For example:
Both activities are relatively natural.
You can't force yourself to fall asleep or become hypnotized. Both experiences have to occur naturally for you to experience them fully.

You can't remember everything that happened while you were asleep or under hypnosis (unless you've consciously recorded these memories). In most cases, people forget the details of their dreams or sessions after they awaken from hypnosis.
They can both help people relax. Hypnosis and sleep are two techniques that can help relax the body and mind, which is the ideal state needed to change habits and learn new skills.
Both hypnosis and sleep provide relief from pain. Some people experience headaches or insomnia, for example, while others may suffer from chronic back pain or arthritis. Pain is reduced and even eliminated in many cases during hypnosis sessions or while you're falling asleep at night.

**Can I Be Under Hypnosis And Have No Memory Of It?**

In most cases, the answer is yes. If you were hypnotized but didn't remember it, you probably went into a natural trance state. This happens to lots of people, including myself. When I was being hypnotized for my weight loss program, I remembered everything that happened up to the point when I was about to go into an altered state. But then came the moment when the therapist said goodbye and left the room. I don't even remember walking back to my chair and sitting down after he left!
I do have memories of being in my office in the evening, with nothing on my mind except finding a nice restaurant for dinner. You see, I had been working all day on a tedious project at work and felt like something nice was for dinner. Then I heard someone talking, "What are you doing? What's the matter? Where are you?" It was my mom, calling from South Carolina. She was a nurse. She said she sensed that something was wrong with me and called to see if I was OK.
What had happened is that I fell asleep in my chair after the hypnotherapy session, and the therapist let me sleep for an hour or two (I have no recollection of sleeping). When he came back into the room, he looked at me with concern and asked what happened. My mom had phoned while I slept and woke me up, so he asked me how long I'd been sleeping. I told him about the session, and he expressed doubt about it.
He disagreed with the therapist's assessment, though I don't recall what he said. But I do remember his tone of voice and his words being very curt and dismissive of my mom's concerns: "Fine, she's fine."

I confronted him with his dismissive attitude. It was not OK to dismiss my mom, especially since she was a nurse and also concerned about me. He explained that this was just the way the field worked, that therapists were trained to bend over backward to convince their patients that they are OK when they are not. But that is not what I experienced, and neither is that the case with other therapists.

I know from personal experience and from conversations with other people who've been hypnotized that hypnotherapists don't dismiss their clients' concerns, especially those who are family members or close friends.

If this sounds familiar to you, then your hypnotherapist may need additional training on handling people who are concerned about a loved one after a session. Also, keep in mind that some people will remember their experiences, others will not, and others may have a different memory of the same experience. Don't worry. It's completely normal and nothing to be concerned about.

**Is Hypnosis A Substitute for Medicine?**

No, hypnosis is not a substitute for medicine. While hypnosis may help people overcome pain or habit problems, it is not a replacement for therapy. If you have a severe medical condition, then hypnosis should not be used in treatment from your doctor! Only your physician is qualified to diagnose your condition and recommend treatment options and manage any additional concerns that you may have. Your doctor can also monitor the effectiveness of any therapy, including hypnotherapy.

If you have a medical condition, be sure that your doctor is aware of your experience with hypnosis. If your doctor approves, you may feel more comfortable discussing any issues or concerns you have during a session. Most doctors are highly supportive of this type of therapy and will be more than happy to talk about it if they know it through another patient or personal contacts.

**Can Hypnosis Be Dangerous to Health?**

If hypnosis were dangerous to health, then the use of electricity would not exist as a form of mass communication and transportation. We would not be using air conditioners or refrigerators, or microwaves because these devices depend upon electricity use. Electricity is a form of energy that can be converted into heat, light, or sound. However, the hypnotist intends to provide positive benefits throughout your body and mind. Hypnosis places you in a relaxed state, which is essential for turning on your brain function.

As long as you seek your goals with sincerity and follow the instructions given by your hypnotherapist correctly and responsibly, then hypnosis will be safe to use for both you and others involved in any session with you.

You may feel unusually tired after your session, so make sure you take plenty of time to rest. Or even better, schedule your session for the evening and make sure that you get plenty of rest throughout the day. That way, if you feel a little tired after the session, it won't be as challenging to get back on track during the day.

# Types Of Hypnosis

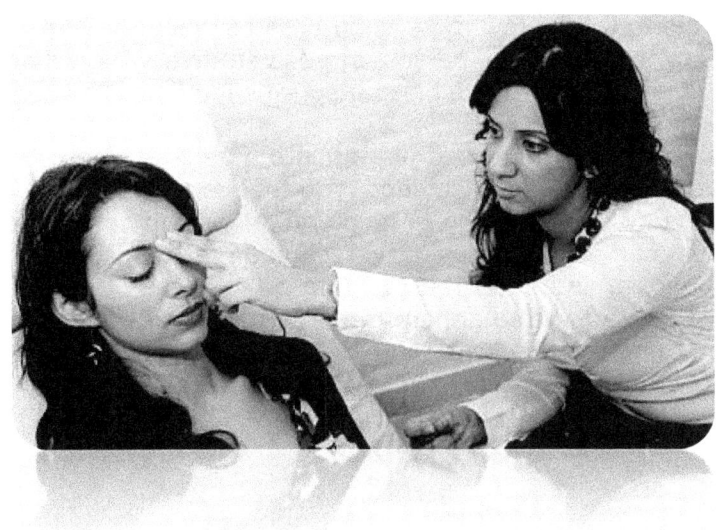

There are different types of hypnosis as well as different techniques that can be used in sessions. Some hypnotists use one or two primary processes, while others specialize in a few methods and practice them regularly over time. The significant types of hypnosis are covered below.

## Basic Hypnosis Techniques

### Generalized Hypnosis

This technique involves using a set of suggestions to help a person relax and fall asleep. The purpose is not to explore serious issues or uncover any subconscious fears or memories but rather to help the person relax and fall asleep quickly. Generalized hypnosis can be found in books, videos, CDs, and online training programs covering these techniques in more detail. For example, the following is an excerpt from one book on general hypnotic induction:

"When you're ready, I want you to take a deep breath and let it out slowly. Then take another deep breath. Once more. And another. And another." The hypnotist would then ask the individual to take a few more deep breaths while the hypnotist counts to twenty. If the person agrees with everything that is happening, you can move on to a specific induction.

For example, if you want to just go into a general sleep state, then you could begin by saying: "You feel very relaxed and sleepy today, so I'm going to help you fall asleep now." The hypnotist can also use this basic technique for relaxation and self-hypnosis, and other reasons that he may see fit. Sometimes it's best to start with a generalized approach and then move on to something more specific.

# Suggested Hypnosis Induction Techniques

The hypnotic induction is the process of helping a person enter into a relaxed state to experience hypnosis. Some people find that self-hypnosis induction is more accessible than other types of hypnosis, mainly because the hypnotist is not present at the time. It can also be considered a type of behavioral conditioning or behaviorism in which you are teaching yourself how to relax and focus your mind on your intentions.

Hypnotic induction should not be confused with the clinical term "hypnosis." Hypnosis is a clinical term to describe when someone has fully relaxed into a deep trance state. In this kind of hypnosis, the hypnotist, or a trained professional trained in hypnosis, guides you from the beginning and checks on you at specific intervals to ensure that you are ready.

In that way, hypnotic induction is different than physiological induced hypnosis. Physiological induced hypnosis involves activating your brain waves through self-hypnotic techniques to relax and achieve an altered state of consciousness (ASC). In hypnosis, you are not learning how to induce a trance state or how to relax. You should not be instructed to do so. If you have an intention to self-hypnotize yourself, then don't! It could be misconstrued as self-hypnosis with deep sleep induction, and that would be dangerous!

Some people learn better from a particular technique than others. For example, some people learn better using a visual method while others know better with verbal suggestions. Some learn best by talking throughout the entire session, while others like the sound of the voice and feel more comforted by it. These techniques have been well studied and tested over time to make them safe and effective for everyone.

## Suggested Hypnosis Induction Techniques

Various suggested hypnotic induction techniques exist, including: Audio-Visual suggestion (using Audio Recordings, Videos, or Illustrations).

This is a type of suggestion where you listen to or watch a video on the subject matter to learn how to relax and trance yourself. You can use audios CDs, videos, illustrations, or other media that you study and watch over and over again until your subconscious accepts them as a way to help you relax.

Some hypnotists may use a moderately heavy regimen of audio-visual suggestions to help clients learn how to trance themselves. For example, the hypnotist may have you watch a video or listen to a CD at least three times over an hour to learn how to trance yourself.

**Mind-Mapping (Visualization)**

This practice is also known as visualizing and is often used in spiritual counseling sessions. This type of hypnosis can be achieved through visualization techniques such as painting or drawing. It can be done on paper, photographs, or any other medium that helps you visualize your intentions clearly and easily.

# Other suggested Hypnosis Induction Techniques

Other suggested hypnotic induction techniques include:

**Thought-Stopping Suggestion (Removing Thoughts)**

This technique is similar to self-hypnotic trance induction. It involves you allowing yourself to become so deeply relaxed that you enter a trance state. Once there, you no longer identify with your surroundings or the people around you, and you then let go of any worries and concerns about what's going on around you. You can also practice this technique by doing self-hypnotic exercises such as finger counting or other relaxation techniques. Once you've reached a deep level of trance, then your thought process begins to slow down and become smoother throughout your body. However, you can let go of complex thoughts to cope with and engage in intense relaxation.

Other suggested hypnotic induction techniques include:

**Hypnotic Suggestion Fluency (beneficial for pre-production)**

You can practice the art of hypnotic suggestion fluency by saying a phrase or sentences out loud. You can practice this out loud or on an inaudible recording (you may want to practice in a room with no distractions). You can also record yourself and play it back while practicing.
Hypnotic Suggestion Fluency is a valuable technique in the pre-production phase of an audio or video hypnosis session. This can help you feel naturally confident while practicing for a session and getting used to being in a trance state before you go into it.

**Omnibus Hypnosis (combining multiple techniques)**

You can combine several suggested hypnotic induction techniques into one session, such as:
Generalized / Relaxation / Self-hypnotic Trance Induction: You learn to relax and fall asleep and calm your mind by practicing

self-hypnosis. Learn how to relax your mind, body, and emotions so that you can achieve an altered state of consciousness (ASC).

**Visualization:**

You relax by using the practice of visualizing where you want to go, what to do, or what you want. You can remember as vividly as possible, being able to feel your feelings and emotions vividly.

**Thought-Stopping Suggestion / Hypnotic Induction:**

This involves removing unnecessary thoughts and allowing yourself to slip into a trance state.

**Mentally Connecting With Ego-Bonding Suggestions:**

You learn to mentally make connections with what you want to help yourself relax and feel safer. You do this by using suggestions like "I am safe, I am so relaxed, I know what to do in any situation."

Omnibus Hypnosis is a type of hypnotherapy that combines multiple techniques to achieve a more profound result. This type of hypnosis is very effective as the mind is more open to suggestions when these techniques are combined.

**Depth Hypnosis (Deep Trance)**

This style of hypnosis involves going into a deep trance state where you can release mental blocks, overcome fears and anxiety, and deal with negative thinking patterns. This level of hypnosis is considered to be one of the most profound and most potent levels.

For example, imagine that you fear snakes, spiders, or a fear of getting sick. When you are pretty nervous, it can prevent you from leaving your home to work or attend a social event with friends. This type of self-hypnosis would help the person conquer this fear by helping them understand what's going on to realize how silly it is.

This type of self-hypnosis involves going into a deep trance state where you can release mental blocks, overcome fears, and build up positive thinking patterns. This hypnosis level is considered one of the most potent levels and the most profound type of hypnosis available.

For example, imagine that you fear snakes, spiders, or a fear of getting sick. When you are pretty nervous, it could prevent you from leaving your home to work or attend a social event with friends. This type of self-hypnosis would help the person conquer this fear by helping them understand what's going on to realize how silly it is.

# Advanced Hypnosis Techniques

Advanced techniques may be considered a derivative of basic hypnosis, and they are similar to depth hypnosis in that they help the person get into a deep trance state. However, advanced techniques are often termed as any technique that is not to fall asleep. Instead, they are meant to help the mind be more open and responsive to suggestions. For example, advanced hypnosis techniques can induce changes in someone's behavior or reduce anxiety.
Counselors and therapists commonly use this method of hypnosis because it allows them to go beyond the surface-level issues present in most people's minds. Hypnosis is a potent tool and the most effective way to supplement psychotherapy.

Advanced hypnosis techniques are used to help you make changes in various things such as:

**Self-Esteem or Self-Recovery (Dissolving Negative Thinking)**

This type of hypnosis helps with the release of negative thoughts that could hold you back from moving forward in your life. You can learn how to use this technique by listening to or reading self-hypnotic books, CDs, and videos to help yourself overcome negative thinking patterns.

# The Power of Guided Meditation

The power of guided meditation is now your key to extreme rapid weight loss. Tapping into one's subconscious is a proven way to access deep-rooted emotions, heal past wounds, and make positive changes.

Let the hypnosis take charge of your cravings, and you'll see what's possible when we work together. Now you can stop feeling like a failure because of your lack of self-control. Get rid of your negative thinking patterns and let your subconscious mind focus on what you want.

My program, beyond weight loss, addresses other aspects of your health. My Audio hypnosis tapes help you gain control of your cravings whenever they arise. You'll stop focusing on food and instead have the discipline to put in the effort required to achieve long-term success.

You'll start with the raw power of my guided meditation audio hypnosis audio files. They will help you reprogram your subconscious to unlock your inner fat-burning furnace and melt away your cravings.

I'll guide you through a modified version of the "Rapid Weight Loss Hypnosis" that's proven effective for women who want to lose weight fast. You won't believe the changes in just two weeks!

That's why I created these special sessions that allow you to get started quickly and begin an amazing new life where you can finally feel light and free.
It's time to let go of your failed attempts at dieting, exercise, and strict eating habits. This is an opportunity to laugh at all of the diets that don't work with our bodies.
You can't out-think an impaired metabolism! You will learn how to use the power of your mind, and I'll show you how to access it right here on this free site.

How do I know? Because I fought the same battle you are facing right now, and now I am a successful certified weight loss coach and hypnotherapist that helps others achieve their goals using hypnosis.

My goal is to help you let go of the past and move into a new lifestyle where you can finally feel light and free. I'll show you how to access your subconscious and use it for good!

I invite you to discover what's possible when we work together in this free guided meditation program. You'll soon realize that there is something much bigger than yourself that controls all of the choices you have made in your life.

Your mind has been robust over the years, but this hypnotic process will allow you to relax, release, and absorb emotions from the deep recesses of your psyche and past.

I'll reveal the secret to tapping into your unlimited potential for creating new belief systems and ways of thinking. I'll show you how you can get the most out of hypnosis so you can begin a new and improved lifestyle.

You already have all the tools inside. They are powerful yet need to be harnessed and focused on for success.
Once you've taken the first step to reach out and discover what's possible, you'll see how quickly results begin to appear.

You will access your mind at will and learn how to use your subconscious mind for good. When you feel those cravings coming on, you'll know what to do.

Once you learn the process I've developed, you'll finally have the skill and knowledge to keep those cravings at bay and leave your addiction to food behind.

Yes, I can coach you through your decision-making process and give you the guidance you need to get started in a new way. You'll be able to see that dieting has its own set of rules that are not always in line with what is best for your body.

I invite you to a new lifestyle where success comes easy because, chances are, we already have all we need within us.

Think of all the things you've wanted that seemed to be out of reach because of your weight problem.

Practicing an extreme rapid weight loss hypnosis meditation program which includes several excellent benefits:

– Unlock the power within to lose weight fast. Fast and easy! Freedom from diets now! – Change your beliefs and old habits now. You will learn how to think thin! – Use your subconscious mind for good! No more feeling guilty for overeating. – Let go of your past eating habits so that you can move on and start over.

– Stop cravings in their tracks! You will never have to dread seeing food again. – Free yourself from the guilt of food. You can stop feeling guilty for overeating. – Change your whole identity and master your weight loss forever!

So many people are now turning to hypnosis to get the help they need. Why not you? You'll be amazed at how easy it is to start losing weight with hypnosis once you remove those negative thoughts and feelings that have been holding you back for so long now.

If you could only see what's possible when we work together, I know it would make a difference in your life forever. It's time to stop feeling that you can't lose weight and start seeing that you can!

You'll see for yourself how powerful your subconscious mind is and how it will always work for you. My free hypnosis sessions have helped so many people, just like you.

The best part of all is the fact that my training program gives you all the tools necessary to start a new way of life full of self-sufficiency and success. You will get to discover how powerful your mind is at helping you go from a failure to success forever. I'll teach you exactly what it takes to transform your subconscious into a successful weight loss partner, where your old habits will become second nature. So much more can be possible when you are using your mind to its most full capabilities.

With the right kind of guidance, way past dieting can become a thing of the past. Weight loss is now so much easier to accomplish, and you won't have to go through all those complicated and painful efforts that used to be necessary for you to lose weight. Now you'll just need a positive attitude and the right kind of support from people in your life who care about your success.

## Who is the best hypnosis coach for me?

A hypnotherapist might be able to guide you through your decision-making process and give you a great deal of help. However, some people are more open to a change in mindset and don't need much guidance at first. You can find great resources online, like this one:

Full list of my weight loss hypnosis sessions here: weight-loss-hypnotherapy-session-list
Whether it's an extreme rapid weight loss program or traditional methods, I'll help you determine which best fits your needs and get the most out of your journey to replace overeating with fasting.

I'm sure you'll be completely confident that your choice is the right one for you, no matter what. You'll be amazed by how fast you can lose weight once you tap into your strengths and allow them to shine.

With my help, all the visions of yourself in a smaller size will become a reality. My sessions are designed to make you want to change, and once that happens, it's only a matter of time until your new lifestyle becomes a natural part of who you are.

# The Power of Affirmation

The power of affirmation can be so strong that you can't even imagine. Many of us have heard the phrase "fake it 'til you make it," which, in truth, it's not such a bad idea. The power of hypnosis is now harnessed with this extreme rapid weight loss hypnosis for women to help them lose weight quickly without dieting or exercise.

You can do things like hypnotizing yourself before eating to curb cravings or even give your mind a boost in confidence by repeating affirmations throughout the day. This is one of those hypnosis scripts that you can use before eating to provide yourself with the extra boost you may need to lose weight.

Simply allow yourself to relax and listen to the hypnosis script repeatedly.

The affirmations will help embed themselves into your mind and give you that little extra kick in the rear when you need it most.

**Extreme rapid weight loss hypnosis for women script:**

(Note: This is a sample script and can be changed as needed. Also, make sure to record this session in a quiet room without any distractions.)

You can do this! Give yourself an extra boost with these affirmations. Repeat them after me while allowing your muscles to relax completely. "I love my body. I love my body. I love my body." (Stress the word "love" when repeating.)

You deserve to feel good about yourself. Feel what it's like to get up in the morning and feel completely refreshed and energized. See yourself looking in the mirror and feeling great about how you look. You're going to keep losing weight and feeling better every single day! "

I'm proud of myself for the progress I've made so far." (Repeat this often!)

"I'm going to eat healthier foods and exercise every single day. I'll make sure that I do these things for myself!" (Repeat this often!)

Now focus on your stomach for a moment. Relax your muscles and allow your mind to become relaxed.
Imagine that all the food is inside your stomach, and imagine that you've just eaten an enormous breakfast. It's now time to eat a snack! Try something healthy like some pomegranate seeds and a small handful of almonds (about 60-80 calories max). "

I'm going to indulge in some healthier snacks like these." (Repeat this often!)

You're on a diet, and you know how to follow it. You're going to reduce the amount of unhealthy food you eat while also being more conscious of what you eat. Remember, every time you eat something that tastes good, remember the fact that it's terrible for you. "

I'm going to eat healthier foods and exercise every single day."

"I'm going to eat a salad for lunch and feel great about myself." (Repeat this often!)
Now focus on your waistline. Imagine that you're wearing your favorite red dress and that it's hugging your waist perfectly! Your waist looks fantastic and sexy! "

I wish my body was like this all the time!" (Repeat this often!)

Breathe in and relax. Breathe deeply in through your nose and out through your mouth. Feel how the air flows into your lungs, down to your chest, and then out again as you breathe in. You're going to feel great about yourself every single day. Imagine that you're at your ideal weight right now. You're wearing your favorite outfit and are feeling amazing! "

I look great in my new black dress." (Repeat this often!)

Feel how good it feels to have lost weight! It's so easy for you because you've been eating so well. You enjoy exercising regularly and always look forward to a brisk walk and jogging session. Now imagine yourself enjoying a bike ride with the wind blowing in your hair!

"I'm down to the weight I've always wanted to be!" (Repeat this often!)

Now focus on your hands for a moment. Whatever weight you've lost, you feel great because your body looks fantastic. You're proud of yourself and don't feel ashamed of what you look like anymore.

"I'm not afraid to show off my new body!" (Repeat this often!)

You know that exercise doesn't have to be a tedious chore that you dread doing every day. You enjoy running, walking, jogging, and doing aerobics because it doesn't feel like a chore. You feel great afterward and enjoy indulging in some healthy snacks!

"I'm determined to exercise." (Repeat this often!)

Congratulations on your weight loss! You should be proud of yourself for accomplishing such a fantastic feat. Allow yourself to get up tomorrow morning and feel energized and ready to take on the world. You're going to love this feeling! "

I'm proud of myself for losing all this weight!" (Repeat this often!)

You've lost weight and look great. Whenever you eat, visualize yourself enjoying smaller portions of healthier food. See yourself fitting into smaller clothes while feeling great about yourself.

"I'm not going to eat as much because I've learned how to control myself." (Repeat this often!)

You look great because it's easy for you to get dressed for the day. After all, you're slim! Skinny jeans and a cute top or two make dressing so much easier for you. You look and feel sexier than ever before.

"I look fabulous!" (Repeat this often!)

Whenever you eat something, remember that it's terrible for you. You love your healthy food now! You always have healthy snacks on hand so that you don't have to stop in between meals. Never skip meals again! "I love how I feel when I eat good food. I never want to eat unhealthily again!" (Repeat this often!)

You feel great about yourself because your new weight has helped you be the person you've always wanted to be! It feels great to accomplish your goals!"

I'm so happy that I lost all this weight!" (Repeat this often!)

Breathe in and imagine yourself enjoying a beautiful day. You're happy because it's such a gorgeous day that you enjoy eating healthier so that you can want the fresh air and sunshine.
"It feels great out today, and I'm going to go for a jog." (Repeat this often!)

You look fabulous when you wear your favorite black dress! Your appearance is always the next important thing on your mind. You feel great and look fantastic!

"I'm glad to be so skinny!" (Repeat this often!)
You look great whenever you go out with your friends. You enjoy going out to dinner with them because you can order something healthy for yourself. You never feel deprived.

"I love going out to eat with my friends." (Repeat this often!)

You're proud of yourself for getting up early and working out in the morning. It feels good to be able to fit into cute workout clothes!
"I'm glad I got up early; I feel great! I'm going to enjoy my breakfast, knowing that it will help me lose weight. " (Repeat this often!)
You love yourself because you're doing such a great job taking care of yourself! You feel proud of your accomplishments.

"I'm so proud that I lost all this weight!" (Repeat this often!)

Breathe in and imagine yourself walking into your favorite store. You know you look your best, and you love being able to wear nice clothes.
You enjoy feeling confident! Your size is just the next thing on your mind because you feel so good being slim.

"I look great and feel great!" (Repeat this often!)

The weather is perfect for wearing a cute sundress! You feel so good being able to wear it since you've been exercising.

"I look so pretty in my sundress; I must be doing something right." (Repeat this often!)

When you walk into the room, you feel very confident because you are proud that you are thin enough to fit into the room! Your hips are small enough that your skin is hanging off of them. Your thigh is too big for your pants, and your toes are too big for your sandals. You're happy because "It makes me happy to get compliments about my weight loss. It makes me happy to fit into my pants!" (Repeat this often!)

"I feel great about being thin enough to fit into this room so well. I just love it." (Repeat this often!)

When you look in the mirror, you feel so confident because your clothes look so good on you! You love the way they look and feel on you, and you know that looking good is the best part of being thin.

"I'm so glad I lost this weight. It is the best!" (Repeat this often!)

You feel so very, very happy about being thin. You feel great! And you know that it will make you glad to live a light life!

"I love being thin, and I'm so glad I lost the weight." (Repeat this often!)

As you become more and more used to these new ways of thinking, you'll find that your confidence in your ability to control your weight will rise. This self-confidence is one of the most valuable traits that you can develop to maintain a healthy weight. Whenever I feel my self-confidence waver, I go back to my mind training notes. You can view the hypnosis technique script I use to remind myself (which is on this page), and it will rekindle my confidence!

I always have a self-confidence booster with me. I don't know how I would handle the confidence that comes from knowing that I can do whatever I put my mind to. I feel great about myself because I am losing weight and looking good! "I feel so good about how healthy eating and exercising have helped me lose weight." (Repeat this often!"

I'm going to keep losing more weight and look and feel better every day!" (Repeat this often!)

And there you have it, a sample extreme rapid weight loss hypnosis for women script.

# Guided Meditation for Weight Loss

Guided meditation for weight loss is the only way to achieve an extreme rapid weight loss and maintain it. Barbara Dehn makes the most popular programs for women and Dr. John Berdahl for men. These programs take just 10 minutes a day, with each meditation designed to be as gentle as possible while still achieving the desired goal of extreme rapid weight loss.
The underlying theory is that rapid weight loss is due to emotional eating and that if this emotional eating is stopped, then the body will use other mechanisms to keep weight on. The weight lost in these programs results from the body being able to burn more calories than are taken in. The secret of this rapid

weight loss is how each person's mind affects how much food they eat and how active they are or don't become.

Guided meditation for women by Barbara Dehn goes like this:

"A week or two before you start your program, you must put aside at least 50 minutes per day of quiet time when you can sit quietly without distractions. During the day, you can take care of your normal household tasks, but during these 50 minutes, you will not be allowed to do anything else. You will not speak, watch television, or use the telephone. You should complete this program for at least three weeks before beginning it."

The guided meditation that Dr. Berdahl uses is called "Let Go of Volume 3" and goes like this:

"Before you begin, let your consciousness become quiet with a gentle stillness in your body and mind. Let go of all thoughts in your mind, so there is only a soft peaceful feeling in you. After you feel that you are no longer thinking, let your mind become quiet in a relaxed state of rest."

Dr. Berdahl explains that the new way of eating works like this:

"For example, let's say Alice is losing weight at her normal rate of two pounds per week. One day she eats a sandwich and now weighs 240 pounds. Another day she eats just half a sandwich and now weighs 200 pounds. The next day she ekes on for two bites and now weighs 180 pounds. And so on, until she finally manages to manage to keep the same weight in her size 12 shoes."

Modern hypnosis for rapid weight loss is an effective way to fit in as little time as possible. And, as with most things that work, the process is not exactly straightforward.

However, when deciding on a hypnosis program for weight loss or anything else for that matter, it is crucial to know what you're getting yourself into and what your objectives are. It's also important to note whether they are reputable and if their support team will be able to answer any questions you may have along the way or help you if the hypnosis program does not meet your specific requirements or standards.

This means researching everything about the program, including what other people say about it, while spending some time learning more about guided meditation.

Weight loss hypnosis is reliable and has been shown to help people lose weight, but like many self-help programs, the program's success largely depends on the individual. Many people claim that it is not practical for them. And while it does work for some, others find that they cannot get past a particular stage.

But what causes one person to be successful with weight loss hypnosis and not another? It all likely depends on several different factors, which are largely unknown or not well understood.

Some people believe that their previous history of dieting, in particular, plays a significant role in their success or failure with weight loss hypnosis. Some people may have always tried to diet before they tried weight loss hypnosis, and thus they were not able to lose weight with dieting.

Ultimately, the reason for the varying success of different people with weight loss hypnosis may all boil down to their subconscious minds. People who can lose weight with weight loss hypnosis have been shown to have an overriding sense of self-control and self-esteem, whereas others have a more chaotic, disordered state of mind. This is likely why people respond differently to this type of program - it's possible that some people need it more than others.

However, it is also believed that while these differences in mind state do exist, they are not necessarily permanent. This is why it's essential to note that weight loss hypnosis is a program that should be used for only a few months at most. That way, the individual can return to their average self-esteem and self-control after a short period.

If you are interested in guided meditation for weight loss, then there are several things you need to consider before starting. One of the most important considerations is whether this will work for you based on your previous dieting history and how much effort you're willing to put into your weight loss goals once you start working with this type of program.

It is also important to note that weight loss hypnosis is not a quick-fix diet program. This means that you should not expect instant results. Instead, you must be willing to invest regular time and effort into your goals if you want them to succeed. It's also important to consider what sort of support system you have in place for yourself. You'll need to motivate yourself and regularly push through any obstacles you may encounter along the way.

Furthermore, it is essential to know how self-consciousness could affect you during your journey using weight loss hypnosis. It could potentially cause them to become less effective for some people.

Hypnotherapy for Weight Loss and Obesity: A Handbook for Practitioners by Richard G. Blomgren, Ph.D. is a good book for anyone wanting to become a hypnotherapist or learning more about the practice of weight loss hypnosis and obesity hypnosis. The book also contains a good overview of the research available when it was published in 1996, along with a thorough section on ethical considerations regarding using weight loss hypnosis on others.

Unraveling The Mystery Of Weight Loss by Dr. Jay Gordon is a very comprehensive book on the role of hypnosis in weight loss. It contains a discussion of the research done regarding weight loss hypnosis and some other topics such as how to conduct hypnosis sessions, body regulation, positive thinking, and more.

Regarding eating and dealing with our weight and our wellbeing, it is imperative to recognize the significance of the psyche body association. Our furious, jam-pressed lives may, in a real sense, be burdening us. In a new survey, 38% of grown-ups detailed eating or indulging in the previous month as a way to manage or evade pressure, and about half of these grown-ups announced these practices in the last week.

If this is an inclination or conduct you can identify with, you're in good company. The uplifting news is: There are steps you can take that might have the option to assist you with overseeing or get thinner, and reflection for weight reduction is one of them.

## Understanding the terminology around meditation for weight loss

Explicit practices and strategies — reflection, careful eating, and intuitive eating — can assist us with learning or relearn how to have a solid relationship with food and how to eliminate any dangerous sentiments we may have encompassing eating. Weight reduction might be a symptom of developing this restored relationship, yet it's significant not to set up shedding pounds as the essential objective. Doing so may oblige us with the goal that we can't eat naturally or in a careful manner.

All things being equal, center around getting a charge out of food sources — eating since you're ravenous, not because you're worried about overwork or family issues and feeling overpowered. You will learn through these practices how to appreciate and cherish your body for everything it can accomplish for you.

Regarding discussing contemplation for weight reduction or reflection for eating and pursuing building up a solid relationship with food, it can assist with understanding what the phrasing implies.

Stress or passionate eating happens when individuals will, in general, eat and gorge due to compelling feelings or emotions, as opposed to reacting to their inner signs of appetite. Some of the time, when we experience clear feelings, these feelings can exceed our actual sensations of completion and satiation, and this can bring about us indulging. In these cases, food is utilized to deal with stress, dulling compelling feelings quickly. Notwithstanding, it's fundamental to recognize that this experience contributes toward sustaining a cycle. Feeling upsetting feelings can prompt gorging, which starts with blame or disgrace, returning to the surface — and not having the option to measure or deal with — negative emotions or stress.

**Five ways meditation can help promote a healthy relationship with eating.**

Contemplation can help us become more careful eaters and even location any emotional eating issues that may endure.

1. Eliminate the disgrace and blame. For the individuals who battle with enthusiastic eating, feeling focused can prompt indulging in mitigating or keeping away from these emotions. This can start guilt or disgrace. Break the cycle. Contemplation not just lessens pressure, which eliminates the trigger in any case. Yet, it likewise assists you with getting more mindful of your feelings and sentiments, so you can perceive those occasions when you're eating when focused on versus when you're eager. Contemplation has likewise been appeared to build our empathy, making us more tolerant of others who may have distinctive body types from our own.

2. Keep up weight reduction and a solid load for the long stretch. Reflection can help your weight reduction endeavors stick. While diet and exercise may help you arrive at your weight reduction objectives, contemplation close by smart dieting and exercise puts forth weight reduction attempts practical.

3. Lower pressure and irritation levels. Contemplation lessens cortisol and C-responsive protein levels, which is gainful to our general wellbeing and may assist us with accomplishing weight reduction and keep a solid weight. Cortisol is related to putting away fat in our mid-region territory (midsection fat) and raised C-responsive protein levels can indicate irritation, which is at the base of numerous infections, including corpulence.

4. Better control of longings. It tends to be hard to battle those exceptional food desires on the off chance that you battle with enthusiasm or gorging Examination shows that care contemplation can help us control passion and overeating.

5. Decline our pressure and nervousness. Getting thinner requires a great deal of exertion, and keeping the load off can be upsetting, in any event, prompting sensations of anxiety. Thirty days of utilizing the Headspace application for day-by-day reflection diminishes pressure by a third, so it is a demonstrated instrument.

# Meditation for Hunger Attack

If you're fighting a hunger attack, meditation might be the key to your salvation. Even 10 minutes of meditation can help produce serotonin, dopamine, and oxytocin, which are all chemicals that help suppress appetite. With these chemicals working on your brain, you will find it much easier to resist the urge to overeat.

In addition to producing these necessary chemicals that suppress appetite, meditation has been found in studies worldwide to have other positive effects. For example, studies show that meditation increases immune function and reduces anger levels while improving self-esteem and overall life satisfaction.

## Double your IQ

This one might seem a bit far-fetched, but research has shown that meditation can increase your intelligence! During one study of young, healthy volunteers, those who meditated regularly were found to have an average IQ of over 10 points higher than the non-meditators. When focusing on the breath, these same meditators achieved patterns of concentration more often associated with advanced levels of yoga practice.

When meditation is practiced in this way, it's often accompanied by other activities such as chanting or yoga, which are thought to amplify the benefits. Meditation can also provide a powerful source of support for mental health conditions that may affect a person's cognitive function.

# Fight Chronic Fatigue

Chronic fatigue is never a fun condition to live with, but if you're tired all the time and struggling to get strong, it can be even more difficult. Fortunately, meditation has been found to help in many of the symptoms associated with chronic fatigue. This includes improving concentration, mood, and quality of sleep and preventing symptoms related to low energy levels.

According to one study, participants experienced improvements in these areas within weeks of beginning a meditation practice….and continued to improve for at least a month after that! Another study found that 60% of chronic fatigue sufferers reported improved quality of life after just two months of practicing yoga or meditation.

**Boost serotonin levels**

Serotonin is the happy chemical that helps us feel good. Well, meditation may help you to make more of it! Research shows that the increase in serotonin during meditation is long-lasting and can last for many weeks after the practice ends. These changes are thought to be responsible for some of the mental health benefits associated with meditation, including improved self-esteem, anxiety reduction, and mood stability.

**Fight manic depression**

Meditation and yoga have also been found to help ease symptoms of manic depression. In one study, mindfulness-based stress reduction (MBSR) helped to reduce depressive symptoms and improve mental health more than typical treatments for this condition. MBSR teaches people how to be more aware of negative thoughts by practicing mindfulness meditation techniques. For these people, the practice of the MBSR meditation proved to be amazingly effective in feelings of depression and anxiety.

As far as yoga goes, my favorite is the Prolojong Yoga App for iPad! I've been using it since August and am thrilled with the results! I was diagnosed with bipolar disorder two years ago and have struggled with mood swings all this time. I started practicing yoga and meditating a few months ago, and this app works! It's effortless, easy to use, and comprehensive. In addition to the morning meditation, which I do every day (for ten minutes), I practice yoga poses anytime during the day. Since I have a busy work schedule, it helps me stay on track with my moods.

**Lower risk of Alzheimer's disease**

There's still much research that needs to be done in this area. Still, studies show that meditation has been found to significantly slow mental deterioration in diseases like Alzheimer's disease. These studies have used a type of meditation called kirtan kriya, which focuses on breathing techniques designed to keep the mind sharp and active. Research shows that practicing kirtan kriya meditation may help to Fight stress, insomnia, anxiety, and depression.

One study found hypnosis to be very effective in treating insomnia, depression, and mild anxiety disorders. In other studies, the use of audio-visual hypnotherapy was found to help control blood pressure and reduce symptoms of depression. The most important thing here is listening to your body and not forcing the meditation if your mind feels like it's not ready for it yet. I've always had a problem with these things because I try so hard to force my mind into doing them when it's just not ready. You can achieve the same benefits of meditation even if your mind is not prepared; IT WILL COME….just give it time.

**Keep your brain sharp as you age**

Since meditation increases your concentration and focus, it's a great way to keep your mind sharp as you age. Research shows that even just eight weeks of daily one-hour meditation sessions can help to improve concentration, memory, and cognitive performance in older adults. Another recent study found that this type of regular mental exercise in older adults (85+) helped increase gray matter density in the brain's hippocampus region and reduce overall cognitive decline over time.

**Practice meditation anytime, anywhere**

Yoga and meditation are not just physical exercises! They are not just good for your body; they're also very beneficial for your mind. It doesn't take much time to do these things either; all you need is a bit of determination and willingness to learn how to do it. I've been using the Prolojong Yoga App for iPad and love it. There are so many things that I can practice at home by myself on my iPad without even wearing pants! It's a fantastic app because you can select from over 50 different poses and customize each session according to your needs (weight loss, stress reduction, pregnancy, depression, etc.). As I said, I've been using this app since August, and my mind is so much more precise and concentrated. I highly recommend it if you would like to get into yoga.

If you're just starting with meditation, please take it seriously and research what works for you. It's essential to find the right type of meditation for YOU because your body can be susceptible to certain things. Please don't take any recommendations from anyone without doing your research first! This goes for yoga too! You should always consult with a knowledgeable health professional before starting these types of practices.

# Tackle Top Weight Loss Limiting Belief

Tackle top weight loss limiting belief in 5 minutes per day!
It's not easy for a woman to lose weight, let alone maintain it. All of the naggings, enticing, and general hard work that dieting requires can get to you. You're tired of the constant fluctuations in your eating habits, feeling hungry one day and stuffed the next. It seems like you're always going in circles, never seeing any results from your efforts. This is why we developed the weight loss hypnosis for women program. It offers you the tools you need to lose weight indeed.

We'll make it easy for you, giving your subconscious mind a toolkit of powerful suggestions that will enable you to shed pounds the natural way. All of our weight loss hypnosis programs are specifically designed for women, considering your body type and how it responds to the various eating plans set out for you. You'll get multiple sessions, each lasting around 20 minutes, as we tailor your program to your unique needs. Usually, a session lasts two weeks, but we can extend this as much as needed if necessary.

# Rapid Weight Loss Hypnosis for Women

## Who Can Benefit from It?

The rapid weight loss hypnosis CDs aim to change a person's eating habits for the better while still allowing them to feel full and satisfied. This audio course is geared specifically toward women who have been unsuccessful with losing weight using traditional dieting methods, such as counting calories and exercising too much. It's designed to help you break patterns of negative thought when it comes to your food. You'll eventually develop a healthy relationship with what you eat and start on your road to success.

Do you want to lose weight but feel like you can't muster up the motivation to change your behaviors? Would you like to break out of your shell and start feeling confident about your abilities? Look no further than the latest weight loss hypnosis CDs. Designed with the busy woman in mind, these hypnotic programs will help you lose weight without sacrificing the things you love to do.

# So How Does Weight Loss Hypnosis Work?

Effective weight loss hypnosis isn't something that comes easy or cheap. It requires you to have a combination of self-discipline and determination for it to work. When you listen to this course regularly, your conscious mind begins to work hand-in-hand with your subconscious mind so that new patterns are formed within your brain.

Do you find it challenging to stick to a diet or exercise program because of that annoying voice in your head telling you that it's not worth it?
If the answer is YES, then this is for YOU. We offer sessions from a highly trained hypnotherapist and nutritionist, which will help you break through these limiting beliefs, build new, empowering thoughts, and sustain weight loss with rapid results. Essentially we will give you the mental tools needed so that making healthy changes doesn't feel like such an overwhelming task.

Hypnosis is a state of focused attention. From this state, you can receive suggestions that can change your thoughts and behaviors to achieve the goals you have set for yourself. You are entirely in control of what offers you choose to accept and reject, so the therapist you choose must have a good reputation for helping people just like you.

As long as your decision-making is not impaired by drugs, alcohol, or pre-existing mental disorders, hypnosis is an excellent way to quickly break through all types of self-imposed limitations on weight management and leading a healthier lifestyle.
You will likely have heard of hypnosis from the popular 60's television show "The Hypnotic Eye."

We are in the process of completing a very successful weight loss hypnosis treatment with weight loss and rapid results that women can use all over the world. Would you like to know more?
Who we treat: This is best suited to women who have tried different diets and exercise programs without much success. It is typically recommended for ages 18 to 65. However, we treat clients of all ages and genres.

We provide the first session lasts around 15 minutes; then, we will continue with telephone sessions at the patient's discretion as part of our ongoing support plan. Our unique hypnosis weight loss program gives you the training to attain rapid results, no matter your initial weight. The purpose is to help you lose weight permanently and lead a healthier lifestyle. The suggested course of therapy is six sessions which can be done in 3 months, although more sessions may depend on the individual.

You will be taught the following: How to overcome your negative perceptions about food and eat, How to improve your self-confidence to become a confident person in general How to break out of bad eating patterns and permit yourself to eat a greater variety of foods.

As you listen over time, the suggestions will eventually become embedded within your psyche, making it easier for you to continue your pattern of healthy behaviors. You'll find yourself being able to go for more extended periods with less food while still feeling full and satisfied. This is a fundamental change from the frustration that it took you so long to achieve. You'll even find yourself losing weight without the constant hunger and cravings you experienced previously. This is the result of those new thoughts having been installed within your brain.

The hypnotic weight loss program will change the way you think about food. Learn how your past experiences in life hold you back from achieving your goals – but don't worry, there is a solution to this!
If you're serious about losing weight and keeping it off, this is the right place.

How it works: We use a special Hypno-program that has been carefully designed to help reprogram your subconscious mind so that you break through the last few blocks that prevent you from seeing results and feel confident with yourself. I give an introduction to the treatment, then spend a few moments introducing you to the process and what's involved before we delve into your imagined weight-loss reality. I gradually guide you into deeper levels of hypnotic trance while trying to instill in you an empowering belief that will sustain any success or failure at losing weight. The subconscious mind then takes the new information and considers it with your past experiences to form a new belief. It is the new belief that provides you with success.

Since your subconscious mind only takes in 20% of your conscious thoughts, this process makes it easier for you to change and effortlessly maintain the behaviors that you want. As a result, we find that even those who have only had 1-2 sessions continue to lose weight without much effort. Some of these clients have even gone on to lose 30 pounds or more in a short period!

**Results: Success stories**

What some of our patients have to say:

" I've been trying for years to lose weight and haven't managed to sustain anything until my friend suggested I try hypnosis. It didn't take much effort on my part, she found a great hypnotherapist who just had me listen to the recording once a day, and it was like a switch being flipped in my head; suddenly, I was eating healthier and exercising regularly! The whole process was so easy that it didn't feel like I was doing anything at all. I still lose weight even when I don't listen to the recording and now have positive beliefs about myself that will sustain any success. Thank you so much!"

- Autumn

"I have a fantastic weight loss success story! I was struggling to lose weight for years, then one day, a friend who works in the health sector recommended hypnosis. I had no idea what it was, but she said that hypnosis had been known to work for everything from psychological issues like anxiety attacks to losing weight. She explained how it works and made me listen to the recording and follow her instructions. After six weeks, I lost 19 pounds and, more importantly, my confidence! My mind had changed about how I feel about myself and also about what is possible. After only one session, my friend suggested that we invest in even better resources to help me with my weight loss goals.

# Healthy Relationship Toward Food

Ultra-low body weight

Enhanced self-image

# Rapid dramatic weight loss in six weeks.

Maybe the most common question we get is what to do when you don't have any willpower. Overcome emotional eating! Lose your love handles! Become a slimmer, happier person in just six weeks! You can do it with this extreme rapid weight loss hypnosis for women. This easy program is designed to help you achieve your goals and live the healthy lifestyle of your dreams. The best part is that we guarantee it will work for you or it's free.

The benefits of rapid weight loss are many. You will achieve your dream weight in just six weeks. As you lose excess body fat and build lean muscle, you will look and feel more attractive. You'll have more confidence and self-esteem, an increased metabolism, and a better quality of life overall. It's a fact: you are not what you weigh on the scale. There is no reason to let your weight hold you back from the life you want or the body you deserve.

What results can you expect from this advanced weight loss program?

You will lose 14 pounds in just six weeks. You will have decreased body fat and increased muscle tone. Your body will be toned and sculpted for a sexy shape and balanced health. Look your best in a bikini or on the beach this summer—not in size 4 or 6! As you achieve your dream body, you'll gain more self-esteem. You'll feel more confident, have a better self-image and get along better with others. You'll find it easier to make decisions.

You will have an enhanced quality of life. You will feel more energetic; you will sleep better and have more energy for your hobbies and interests. Ego depletion is a beautiful feeling! You'll appreciate yourself more, which means you'll take better care of yourself and live a healthier lifestyle. You can even lose weight without dieting or exercising—you just need to follow the program correctly and quickly!

**What are the risks?**

Your weight loss can be fast—but it's also safe, easy, and permanent. It's easy to follow because you don't have to change your lifestyle at all. You don't need to diet or exercise, and you won't put yourself under a lot of stress. It's that easy to lose weight quickly with this program.
Rapid weight loss hypnosis interferes with the regulation of emotion and behavior through the subconscious mind. Here are some of the changes associated with extreme rapid weight loss hypnosis:

**The attraction mechanism for food is disrupted**

The rigidity of thinking, judgment, and decision making suffers [inability to think about long term consequences]

**The unconscious motivation for eating is decreased.**

Calories are seen as an "enemy," and eating is viewed as immoral. This is an extremely dangerous mindset for weight loss! People may become obsessive about their weight and health. They may avoid everyday meals, eat mainly low-calorie food or eat aphrodisiacs or stimulants to increase their metabolism (despite the damage this causes to the body). This leads to an increase in free radicals in their bodies and a decrease in antioxidants leading to cellular degeneration.

A diet high in stimulants can also cause damage to the kidneys. Weight loss with this program can also lead to a state of hyperactivity in the muscle cells. This can cause fatigue, weakness and lead to a decrease in overall energy.
In extreme cases, this leads to serious health problems such as sleep apnea, heart failure, chronic fatigue syndrome, and cancer. Long-term weight loss is associated with various medical issues, including hypoglycemia (low blood sugar), impaired glucose tolerance, stomach complaints, and kidney disease. These problems are compounded by the fact that some people start with an inherited predisposition towards cancer of the breast or prostate gland.

Another possibility is that weight loss can cause psychological damage to other areas of life, affecting relationships, careers, and everyday living.
The "weight loss" itself can also cause psychological damage as a result of the following:

People are less likely to maintain stable weight loss.
People experience the initial weight loss as a reward for their effort. Still, they lose motivation very quickly and eventually achieve rebound weight, even if they had a lot of initial inspiration. This is because their real goal is to look good rather than try to feel good.

Even if people lose weight initially, they don't keep it off and suffer more permanent health consequences. It's tough to keep weight off in the long term.
Consult your doctor before starting this program. Rapid weight loss brings up health risks. You need to be aware that these changes can happen, and it's essential to consult your doctor before commencing this type of program.

**How to start having a good relationship with food?**

It's one thing to expect change — and it's another to attempt to get change going effectively.

In the first place, recall that you're your individual. You have your own set of experiences with food, your food inclinations, and each option to explore this excursion such that suits you.

Beneath are some helpful hints. Consider them, and attempt them. They've been tried out by a gathering of individuals on the planet, and they've been found to work.

To begin with, get into the habit of recording what you eat each day. Most folks aren't familiar with this activity, yet it's crucial. In any case, once you begin doing it regularly, you'll see that upon your come back to the sheet from time to time during the day – late in the afternoon or night – that you'll have a more drawn out picture concerning what you're eating routine truly is in any given week – or month for that matter.

Next, make an earnest effort not to eat in front of your TV, PC or tablet screen, or telephone. If you regularly watch TV while eating, for example, you'll incline toward what was on the net. Also, if you frequently snack while texting or emailing or on the web, it's an intelligent thought to disengage from these things and to begin eating at a table with a plate with just a couple of simple items on it.

After that, make an effort not to keep any food or treats within your line of sight anymore. On the off chance that they're nearby, you'll have no alternative but to look at them repeatedly. Disengage from chocolates and cookies and whatever other bounty in your home and at work.

Don't let all this be a drawback. Set up an eating routine that works for you. Begin to notice what feels comfortable and natural. There's nothing like observing your plate fill up effortlessly – have some chicken or white meat mince, a couple of green vegs, some fresh greens (not pasta), and a piece of fruit, or so on.

If you need to take it to the following level, add extra stuff – for example, broccoli stir-fry in place of noodles — whatever works for you will feel best.

Save the specific topic of food as the last thing you do that day, and just before bedtime, has come as a separate activity. You will find that you are more likely to eat healthily when you are well-rested, and it's more appropriate that way.

If you have a few pounds to lose, do not be daunted by it. It happens for reasons of innumerable flavors and tastes and all the things we need and physical ailments in our bodies. The first and most imperative step is to change your eating behavior, which means taking in fewer "junk" calories.
Eat smaller amounts than before, but frequently throughout the day. It should never be that you are satiated at one sitting. If you are, you will not take in essential elements and nutrients that your body requires.

When you have a craving for something sweet, always seek out an alternative sweet snack instead. Limit your carbohydrate intake and eat more protein and fiber. This will help to prevent a surge of insulin and will keep your energy levels stable. Snack on nuts, fruits, or vegetables with cheese or yogurt if possible. One thing to avoid is hard candy; this is how people become addicted to sugar in the first place!

BREACKFAST consists of two bowls of oatmeal with added chia seeds or flaxseed oil or both (the real stuff). This is heart-healthy oatmeal, high in fiber, and when topped with berries, it's delicious.

LUNCH is usually either a salad or leftovers from the night before (the risk of cross-contamination is lower because I clear the kitchen down to my new kitchen table) or simply two baked chicken breasts over salad greens. This change in diet from the night before makes me feel healthier and more energetic all day.

DINNER is a magical time for me because it means I can eat almost whatever I want! Again, portion size matters. After dinner, I like a piece of dark chocolate on top of some Greek yogurt with raspberries on top. This is the treat that makes me feel healthier.

About exercise, I like to do a few jumping jacks and other easy stretching exercises before I start my day, at least 5x a week.

This is short and sweet, so it doesn't take much time at all. A bonus of this little routine: it gets my metabolism going in the morning and helps me remember why I love being healthy today!

This has been my strategy for weight loss (and prevention of weight gain) for years now. I've had to tweak it a bit with marriage, babies, and life in general – but the same strategy has won me the weight I want time after time.

You may have various approaches to weight loss that you would like to incorporate into your plan. You can also explore more of my strategies here.

Your health care professional should know that your body doesn't care about one's goal weight or shape. Healing starts with the mind and heart!

Dr. Jim Forde is a Naturopathic Doctor and Certified Hypnotist with over 30 years of experience helping people turn their lives around for the better. He specializes in helping people lose weight and regain their health. He is a former NFL player who spent ten years playing in the Canadian Football League. He has also played on the professional level in Europe, where he developed his expertise as a weight loss expert.

As an IWLPA Certified Professional Hypnotist, Dr. Forde has developed comprehensive weight loss programs using Neuro-Linguistic Programming techniques (NLP), Body Psychotherapy, and NLP-X (the X represents both Chinese medicine and Mind Control).

Dr. Forde's weight loss program has helped many people lose weight and regain their health. His techniques are safe, natural, and easy to follow. They will help you develop new habits, lose your love handles and deal with emotional eating, so you have more strength over food. This will give you increased energy, vitality, self-esteem, and confidence in a relatively short period. This is average rapid weight loss that lasts because it is sustainable.

# Overcome Emotional Eating

Overcome emotional eating and lose weight by listening to a hypnosis session specifically designed for women. This hypnosis recording has been designed specifically for women who want to overcome emotional eating and lose weight.
It explores all the reasons why you might overeat and helps you identify your triggers. The recording also includes affirmations that will help motivate you with statements like "I am a smart woman who is worth my time" and "I am strong enough to resist temptation."

Rapid weight loss hypnosis has been shown to release endorphins, which make us feel full faster. This, in turn, decreases appetite, making food less tempting when we're trying to stay on track.

Extreme rapid weight loss hypnosis for women includes a session of 10-20 minute hypnotic audios, which can be listened to at your leisure. The entire self-help program is designed to help you achieve and maintain a better and healthier relationship with food by eating more slowly and savoring your meals.

Women tend to be emotional eaters, which is why they struggle with their weight; other causes are work stress, bad relationships, lack of self-confidence, and many other related issues. These issues need to be taken care of to create a weight loss hypnosis program specifically for women. This program includes audios designed to help you overcome your emotional eating habits and reject the food that has been used as a substitute or reward for starting over again.

The recording sessions are designed to help you change your relationship with food by making you more aware of how and when you eat. They will make you notice that the amount of food you eat has more to do with how your day went rather than how hungry you are.

The audios will help you notice how your body is affected by eating certain foods and choosing a healthy alternative to keep your energy levels up, and help you feel great about yourself. This leads to a better self-image and improved self-confidence, which will ultimately cause you to rely less on food for comfort.

The program includes:

Your subconscious is very powerful, and the reprogramming sessions included in this program are designed to enable you to tackle the issues that have caused your weight gain and make positive changes in other areas of your life.

By listening to these programs, you will:

– Start taking better care of your body.

– Enjoy eating more and quitting emotional eating.

– Find yourself consuming fewer calories overall.

Extreme rapid weight loss hypnosis for women will help you understand how food affects your moods and how you can break the cycle of emotional dependency on food that causes so many women to struggle with their weight. This new awareness will help you make confident decisions about your diet and achieve long-lasting results.

The self-hypnosis CDs in this program are the only ones that specifically target women. Most other programs on the market for women focus on weight loss but do not address emotional eating as a problem that needs to be overcome.

This program is focused on helping you actively resolve your relationship with food and gain a greater understanding of why you are emotionally dependent on it. This knowledge will empower you to choose healthy alternatives to comfort and help you achieve and maintain a better and healthier relationship with food and your body.

"Weight loss hypnosis program for women contains 10-20 minute audios, which can be listened to at your leisure." Once bought, wait for download instructions, which may take up to 24 hours.

If you have been struggling with your weight for a long time or want to get rid of guilt around food, emotional eating, and weight gain, then Hypnotic Gastric Band for women is the right program.

If you are like many women, you wake up one day and decide it is time to lose weight. You start a new diet and exercise routine with the best of intentions, but then life gets in the way, and you end up regaining all of your lost weight plus more! Weight loss hypnosis for women will eliminate your emotional eating and help you reach your goals faster than ever.

Here is what you will gain by listening to the Extreme rapid weight loss hypnosis for women:

-       A recording session that includes hypnosis and subliminal suggestions to help you lose weight fast without dieting

-       Subliminal suggestions designed to reprogram your negative body image and eliminate your emotional eating

- Regular, relaxing audios that will help you eat less without having to resort to drastic measures like diet and exercise

- Hypnotic audios that provide natural methods of losing weight while boosting your metabolism

- Improvement in the other areas of your life by eliminating bad habits, stopping procrastination, and increasing your self-confidence

By using these potent weight loss techniques combined with your determination and motivation, you can easily succeed. The audios provided in this program include weight loss hypnosis for women designed to help you lose as much as 15 pounds in a month while preventing you from gaining the lost weight back.

This is not about losing weight quickly and then picking up where you left off; this is about losing all of your excess fat and replacing it with a healthy muscle tone. The audios will help you enjoy a diet-free diet that will change your life forever.

To get the most out of your weight loss hypnosis for women CD or MP3, we recommend you listen to it daily. This will help you to overcome the negative mindset which can sabotage your weight loss program. The effects of a positive attitude are greater than those who just listened once or twice.

The following suggestions are helpful for men and women:

1. Go to bed earlier; avoid sleeping with a television, computer, or another electronic device in your bedroom. The light emitted from these devices decreases melatonin levels resulting in difficulty falling asleep or staying asleep. Like when you sleep without putting on pajamas, don't go to bed without putting on the headphones of weight loss hypnosis mp3 download.

2. Avoid eating after seven o'clock at night; not only will you gain more weight, but it blocks your chances of reaching a deeper level of sleep which is when the unconscious mind is the most accessible for the suggestion.

3. Avoid strong spices, hot foods, and coffee after seven o'clock in the evening. Coffee and tea should be taken in the morning BEFORE breakfast or when you are NOT hungry.

4. Minimize alcohol intake; this is an excellent idea if you have been drinking before trying to sleep at night. Alcohol suppresses melatonin release, which increases hunger for food and sugar metabolism since it stimulates the digestion of fat. Alcohol also results in a temporary boost of leptin, which then decreases appetite for food and sugar metabolism and decreases the production of testosterone, which helps inhibit eating behavior and regulate serum glucose ridges (a measure of blood sugar) in your brain.

5. Increase the amount of time you spend in the sauna or steam room and increase stretching. The increase in temperature causes an increase in thermogenesis and increased blood circulation to your abdominal organs, which quiets down hunger for food and sugar metabolism.

6. Exercise daily, especially cardio exercise; regardless of how active you were before starting weight loss hypnosis for women, you will be shocked at how much better your health will be by following this advice that is entirely safe to follow even if you have been a passive person before starting weight loss hypnosis.

7. Drink the right amount of water; 8 glasses of water daily is recommended for women.

8. Be sure to do your weight loss hypnosis recording 5-6 times a day; don't worry, it will NOT make you lose weight any faster or any more than the three times a day that it is recommended, and there are no harmful effects whatsoever on losing weight by listening to the weight loss hypnosis mp3 download first thing in the morning, last thing at night, whenever you have an appetite for food or sugar metabolism, and whenever you are feeling hungry or craving sweet foods.

9. Avoid caffeine after 7 p.m., the coffee you have after dinner, or the cup of tea or soda you have in the afternoon.

10. Don't worry about losing weight too quickly; it should happen naturally because of the health and emotional benefits that weight loss hypnosis for women has for you.

11. Keep a journal of what foods you are eating and how much you are eating; this will help you keep track of how many calories

would make it easier to lose weight and stay healthy once you're done with your dieting program.

12. Avoid eating for two hours before going to bed; this helps your body digest the food quicker and better, especially if you are listening to weight loss hypnosis mp3 download, and it will help in weight loss for women not only by preventing heartburn but also by getting the right amount of sleep that you need.

13. Donate old clothes; they might be hanging on to the fat picture of yourself, making it hard for you to adjust to your new body that you would get after losing weight with weight loss hypnosis.

14. Make sure that you drink plenty of water and avoid caffeinated drinks after 7 p.m.

15. Don't limit your exercise; walk for at least 10 minutes daily; anything more than that is better because it can improve your health by preventing high blood pressure, heart disease, and overweight and helping you lose weight.

# Healing Your Body

Healing your body, your mind, and your life.

- You can finally stop thinking about being fat and start living a healthy life.

- You will be able to eat whatever you want without gaining weight.

- Most importantly, you'll regain your confidence and, in time, find love with someone who respects you for who you are.

But all this is possible because of hypnosis (or neuro-linguistic programming) - a healing process that the medical community has used to treat everything from war wounds to mental disorders and smoking cessation, pain relief, weight loss, and more.

Using hypnosis, you will be able to move past your issues without even thinking about them. If you choose, you'll be able to make positive changes that fulfill your every desire.

**What is Rapid Weight Loss Hypnosis?**

Rapid Weight Loss Hypnosis (also called "Rapid Weight Loss Technique") is based on the idea that people who are overweight or obese are hypnotized while they eat a minimal amount of food and lose a lot of weight in a short time. In other words, this technique is a lie. It doesn't work and shouldn't be used for weight loss purposes, even though it has caught the medical community's attention.

**The True Story Of Rapid Weight Loss Hypnosis**

Rapid Weight Loss Hypnosis is the story of a young woman who fell prey to a well-meaning but deceptive weight loss technique. I won't name her or her town because she chose not to come forward to speak about her experience, hoping that she could help others learn from her mistake.

It all started when she was 17 years old when she weighed more than 200 pounds and had been bullied and taunted for that weight for as long as she could remember. She had tried everything from diet pills and diet programs to exercise plans and various other methods with limited success.

One day, she was approached by a young man who claimed he could help her lose weight. He told her to go to a particular website and purchase a program to help her learn hypnosis for weight loss. She did not question the website's authenticity or ask many questions because she believed this was her chance to be thin.

She entered her credit card information at the site and purchased the program. When she received it, the young man told her to go to another website that supposedly had guided hypnosis programs, but it turned out to be one of the hundreds of rogue scam sites that promise quick weight loss with no effort whatsoever on your part.

She purchased the program on that site, again paying with her credit card. She downloaded the program and tried to listen to it, but she could not hear anything. She thought this was a problem with her computer, so she asked her mother to listen to it on her laptop. Her mother did not hear anything either. But that didn't stop the girl from believing that the young man was going to help her lose weight - even though she couldn't find a way to contact him or anyone else who might be able to offer support.

After a few short months, she had lost about 10 pounds - and then it all stopped. She had no idea how to get it going again, so she asked the man who sold her the program for help. He told her to go to another website that supposedly offered support. She did, and she was asked for her credit card information. She handed over her credit card information, but - again - nothing was downloaded.

So she went back to the young man who sold her the program and asked for help once more. He told her to go back to another website that supposedly provided support, and he gave her a long list of specific instructions on what programs and products she should buy - each at a different site than the last one.

Each time she bought a program, she was asked to pay with her credit card. Each time, the program stopped working after a few days - and each time, she believed that if only she found the right site or the right digital product, it would help her lose weight and be happy.

Finally, she got fed up and asked for help from the support staff at the last site on the young man's list of recommended locations. The support staff told her that all this was just a scam - an elaborate scam that made money for everyone involved. She tried to get her money back from all of them, but of course, it was too late. She never did lose another pound.
By the time she was finished paying for all those different products and programs, she had spent more than $5,000 - and that was just on the digital products.

**Who Is To Blame?**

Of course, this young girl is not to blame for her unfortunate experience with Rapid Weight Loss Hypnosis. She grew up with a weight problem that made her feel less desirable, less attractive, and self-conscious in social situations. She was desperate to find a way to lose weight and regain her self-confidence.

The young man who sold her the program was not at all malicious in his intentions - even though he did make money from these scams in addition to having his name associated with them. He also felt that he might be helping others to lose weight when he sold them those programs. And the people who hosted scam sites offering these products were just trying to make an honest living. After all, they did not know if the digital products they were selling worked or not.

The problem is that everyone involved with this type of digital program was caught up in the mob mentality of those who refuse to stand up against scams like Rapid Weight Loss Hypnosis - and refuse to stand up for those they victimize.

Remember, this young girl did not get help from anyone other than those who sold her programs and websites promising weight loss via hypnosis (the support team at the last site she tried). No one in the medical community stepped in to help her or any of the others who bought these programs, and no one on her family or friend circle was willing to step up and offer helpful advice.

The people who could have helped her were too concerned about their self-interests to challenge the status quo. They also did not want to give up a chance for easy money if their sites got more traffic from people like this young girl. So they kept quiet and kept taking money - and refused to turn anyone away, no matter how many of them were ripped off by these scams.

**Why Does This Keep Happening?**

We live in a world today where the people who have money and power in the medical field face more challenges than ever before. People are beginning to question the value of many drugs, treatments, and procedures that their doctors prescribe for them - and asking whether or not they need those things. They are also becoming more suspicious of their health insurance providers, who try to push them into expensive procedures, medicines, and surgeries that they think they don't need. And we see even more questions about the quality of care at hospitals and medical facilities across the country.

In other words, people are questioning everything about modern medicine these days - including its diagnostic abilities.
Most people do not want to be part of a medical system that runs on blind faith and increased profit margins, but they don't know where else to turn. And rather than step up to help, they keep buying from these programs and supporting their businesses by purchasing the products.

I'd also like to add that many other false claims made by those who sell hypnotic weight loss programs are equally as damaging because they leave you feeling depressed or desperate about your situation - which is a self-fulfilling prophecy. Make sure that you research your options and weigh the true benefits of each program carefully before deciding to purchase any type of hypnosis product.

Hypnosis is not meant as a standalone program for weight loss. It's only one part of the equation that will help you lose weight - and it shouldn't be used to replace a diet and exercise program either. You will find that hypnosis encourages you to eat healthier, move more, and develop an overall lifestyle plan.

But I wasn't just skeptical about all of these so-called "bundles" or "systems." I was also unsure about the quality of the products being offered. I've reviewed hundreds of weight loss products, including hypnosis programs, and self-hypnotists create the vast majority with very little or no training. I'm sure that you've read my reviews of some of those products, and I don't say this to promote a bias against self-hypnosis products. I just wanted to point out that it's essential to do your homework before investing your hard-earned money into any product that promises massive weight loss success in a short period. Sometimes you may find that a particular diet or supplement will work around the clock, but other times there might be times where it doesn't. The important thing is to prepare yourself mentally and physically before using a supplement or specific diet regimen. This will help prevent any frustrations that may come from trying to lose weight too fast.

# Is Weight Loss Surgery Possible?

I have heard this question more than once from people who are resistant to the idea of weight loss surgery even though it seems like a straightforward solution for those struggling with obesity. I know what it's like to be overweight and struggle with constant anxiety about taking on the responsibility of losing weight through diet alone.

However, weight loss surgery is a far cry from something that should be considered lightly. It is very invasive, to say the least, and could have severe long-term side effects for those who choose to undergo it.

If you happen to be in the excellent physical condition and still overweight, then I would highly suggest that you consider fasting or eating tiny amounts of food for several days before and after the surgery.

This may be more beneficial in the long run than the surgery itself. If you aren't an athlete, then fasting would most likely not help you lose much weight because your body would not have to work as hard to burn calories while fasting.

This would also help build up your body's ability to burn fat while you are still eating because the body would be more efficient at burning fat after being fasted for a short time.

If you decide on going through with weight loss surgery, then I would recommend that you get all the information you can and even look into some of the cost-saving health options that might not involve surgery.

There are many ways to lose weight quickly, avoiding dealing with the complications of blood loss, infection, and other possible risks of surgery.

Losing weight is not something that should be rushed - especially if it involves any type of surgery.


Successful Experience of Hypnosis Weight Loss
I had an out-of-body experience where I saw myself, mother earth, and the atmosphere. It was very peaceful and relaxing.

Suddenly, as if from behind me or in front of me, came two other beings, one on either side. One was more to my right side and the other to my left. I felt like I could see them, but then again, they were just beyond my peripheral vision and not really clear, but up close while looking at me, they were there.

I had a feeling of peace and love. It was very comfortable, and I felt safe. They were smaller beings but with much wisdom about my life. I can say about this experience that it was like nothing that I had ever experienced before. It's not something you read about in books or see on tv, but indeed, something like this happens to people every day, or at least during an out-of-body experience.

During one hypnosis experience, his mother appeared, dressed in white, and spoke to him using telepathy. He says she told him to relax and be fine after a few words from her. After a few minutes, he found that he was able to communicate with her by telepathy.

I had a friend with me, and he was like a devil on one shoulder and an angel on the other. I heard the devil say in my voice, "You'll never make it," etc., and the angel saying, "Keep holding onto The Father." This went on for a few minutes, with my friend sitting there watching all of this take place inside of me. It seemed like an eternity, but I later found out that it was only about 5–7 minutes long. It felt like hours because it was so vivid and intense at the same time.

I was very close to feeling the Presence of God during this experience. I felt His Presence and a sense of His Love and that He wasn't angry at me at all. He was just trying to tell me what I needed to hear, which is apparent after reading this article. After a while, we were able to talk without using words because the telepathy came through so well.

I wondered why God would come out in such a manner when I was not even religious, but now I am shocked that such an occurrence took place for someone who does not believe in God or his existence. I'm sure it has to be something greater than myself. I have read about similar experiences and that Jesus, or God, was there. Some people have even told me that they had met him too, but I am trying to figure out whether they did or not. It's just amazing how strong our subconscious minds are.

You are your own worst enemy. You struggle with your subconscious mind, and it keeps you stuck in the same old cycle of self-hatred, lack of self-love, fear, guilt, shame, and unworthiness. It will keep you unable to make progress in life until you finally wake up and realize that you have so much inner power within yourself.

Don't let others' beliefs affect your perception of yourself as worthless. We all have these failures in life, and we go through the motions as if it was just average, but it's not normal at all. No one is supposed to go through life thinking that they are worthless. What you are experiencing is not normal; it's a reaction to the subconscious mind.

You want to make progress in life, then what you need to do is start setting yourself up for success instead of having a feeble mind telling you that you are not deserving of anything good in life. You are worthy and will find that your success habit will begin with small steps. Don't go out there and try to do everything all at once because that's when things don't work out so well. You have to take small steps and gradually build up your self-esteem as an individual by putting yourself first more often than not. Giving yourself what you want is much better than giving to others because that is the best way to express your gratitude.

# Successful Experience with Hypnosis Weight Loss Story

**The First Step for People Who Want To Have Successful Weight Loss Experience**

First, it's important for those who are in the process of achieving their weight loss goals to realize that they should know what they want and where they want to take their lives. It will make a big difference if you have taken off some weight and have managed to keep it off or if you were never able to lose it in the first place. In any case, you need to know what your ultimate goal is and what you need to do differently to achieve your goal.

Another thing that you should do if you want to lose weight is to develop a plan that includes everything that will be necessary for your weight loss journey. The important thing here is not only coming up with the project but also following it carefully so that you do not stumble on any obstacle or setback along the way.

It is essential for overweight people and wants to lose weight to know that they need to allow themselves time for their bodies to heal because it will take a while before they see significant changes on their body. However, the good thing is that they will not experience many of the unpleasant side effects such as headaches and fatigue that they experienced before while taking other weight loss products, including supplements.

The first step for people who want to lose weight is to set their mind on what they want because it can help them achieve better results along the way. It can also make it easier for them to follow their plan because their ultimate goal would be to see what they need to do to reach their target.

If you have a plan that will help you lose weight, then it's time to execute the plan. Every step you take from this point on will reward you with success, so make sure that you never lose sight of what you want and where you want to go in life because your weight loss goal is the same as your ultimate goal in life.

**How To Lose Weight & Change Your Life Forever**

Imagine seeing yourself healthy and fit. Imagine yourself looking great, being youthful, feeling good about yourself - and an energy level like never before! Imagine not only losing 5 – 15 pounds but so much more!

Still, sound like a dream? Well, don't get too excited yet... Successful weight loss is a realistic goal – and with the proper techniques, tools, and know-how, it's possible for millions of people every year!

How To Lose Weight & Change Your Life Forever. You can lose weight fast! Just think of it this way: Is there anything that would make you more excited than reaching your ultimate goal? Nothing! Not only are you going to look great, but you're going to be so much healthier and happier as well.

So what's stopping you from getting started on your journey? Perhaps lack of motivation or the fear of looking like a "dieter"? Don't worry about that! And don't worry about feeling anxious either – what people will say or think is irrelevant at this point... So let's get down to business! It's going to be fun! And there's NO reason you can't achieve your dream weight...

Keeping a journal is a significant weight loss and healthy living tool in itself. However, to ensure that you can keep track of your growth and progress, it is recommended that you also invest in a quality body scale. The model we recommend is the EatSmart Precision digital bathroom scale here.

When we are trying to lose weight, we tend to think about the food we are eating rather than paying attention to other things like exercise, supplements, or other health-related items.

The truth is that when we pay attention to what we are eating, it can help us realize how much of an impact the food we are eating has on what our body is doing and how our body reacts to certain things.

Many people who eat a healthy diet and get regular exercise can still have a hard time losing weight simply because they are not paying attention to the other aspects of health essential for good health. The great thing about paying attention to your health beyond just food is that it will begin to give you more energy, increase your stamina so you can continue exercising, make you more mentally alert, and even help you in your sleep as well.

# Step by Step Approach for Beginners

Step by Step Approach for Beginners, we want to make your life easy and give you everything you need to live a healthier lifestyle. That's why we have created a 10-step program that will help you start living healthier without needing any training or expensive equipment. All it takes is a few days of commitment—giving up your favorite foods, avoiding the gym, or even taking care of an exercise routine—and then the rest is simple!

STEP ONE: Beat the Busy Workload

It's not easy to find time for yourself when work is always beckoning you from afar. But taking just 5 minutes out of your day for stretching exercises can be enough to keep you going throughout the whole day. Just think of it as the first step to a healthier life!

STEP TWO: Get a Good Night's Sleep

It's no secret that sleep and exercise are essential for creating a healthy lifestyle. That's why we recommend you get at least 7 hours of good quality sleep every night. We also encourage you to try going to bed early, so you don't have to worry about oversleeping and being late for your day's work.

STEP THREE: Eat Healthier

We know it's not easy to give up eating your favorite foods, but in times like these, we ask you to keep a positive attitude and think about all the delicious dishes you can eat when you've lost some weight. If you need some motivation during this process, remember that your health comes first—and that's the most important thing!

STEP FOUR: Get Some Sunshine!

Just because winter is coming doesn't mean you can hide from the sun! We recommend taking a walk outside every once in a while for at least 15 minutes of good quality sun exposure. This will make sure your body stays working correctly and doesn't go into depression.

STEP FIVE: How to Eat Like the Hippies

It turns out that hippies were right all along! That's why we want to give you some tips on how they eat their meals and how you can also follow their example! For example, eating a big salad for breakfast is much better than always having a bowl of corn flakes with milk.

STEP SIX: Working out at Home Instead of the Gym

Gym memberships are expensive and not worth paying if you're just going to use them a couple of times this year, right? So why don't you try working out at home instead? If your home is small, try using the stairs instead of the elevator. At the very least, try walking up and down the stairs a couple of times after dinner.

STEP SEVEN: How to Develop a Healthy Relationship with Food

We all indeed love food, but if you want to be healthy, you'll have to learn how to fight against food cravings. There are many tips and tricks from nutritionists that you can use to gain more control over yourself when eating food. For example, you can keep a food journal to remember everything that is going into your mouth.

STEP EIGHT: Avoid the Gym

Many people find it hard to work out at home because they don't have any equipment readily available. Our advice is simple—just forget about the gym and throw away all your old equipment! This will give you clear space in your home for doing all sorts of new activities like gardening, playing with animals, or even exercising in the comfort of your own home!

STEP NINE: Reinforce Your Exercises!

It's so easy to neglect one's own body when it comes to working out. That's why we recommend you pay a visit to the gym, TAKE YOUR TIME, and convince yourself that what you're doing is real.

We also suggest you bring a friend who will push you to your limits—and who can take pictures to document your progress!

STEP TEN: Ayurveda

Most people think that Ayurveda is all about herbs and natural remedies. But this old school of medicine uses a lot more than those things! For example, it focuses on building up the body for good health. That's why we want to show you how specific exercises take less time than others depending on how much weight they will leave behind when they are finished.

# Ayurveda Exercises

STEP ONE: Stretch your arms and legs.

This one is the easiest one out there, and it takes just a couple of minutes of your time! While you're sitting down or standing up, stretch each of your limbs in all directions—you'll see how good that feels for you.

STEP TWO: Work on your stomach.

Stomach exercises are not as easy as they sound, but if you feel like you've done everything else, then why not give it a shot? Lie down on the ground or a yoga mat with your hands behind your neck and do some simple exercises to lift your chest and run in place. These exercises can also be done with the assistance of a friend.

STEP THREE: Work on your chest and back.

When you're standing or sitting down, lift one of your arms above your head and hold it there for as long as you need to get a good stretch in. Then, repeat the same process with the other arm. Also, place your hands on your hips and twist them around until they feel good again!

STEP FOUR: Work on your legs and arms.

If you're sitting down, choose a position where you can work out both of your legs at once. For example, position your feet in a "V" and lift one leg while you twist it in the opposite direction of where you are standing. Repeat this process with the other leg!

STEP FIVE: Workout on all fours.

If you're not comfortable doing exercises on your back, then work out your stomach and chest and do them lying down on the ground while holding your stomach. Also, keep one arm raised high in the air, and the other arm stretched out flat to your side. Do everything very slowly!

STEP SIX: Work out on all fours.

This time, instead of keeping both arms flat to the ground, keep one of your arms as flat as you can and raise the other arm. In this position, you should try to move your arm in circles around your head. This exercise is excellent for your health because it stretches out all of your muscles!

STEP EIGHT: Get on all fours.

After you've worked out everything else and feel like you're about to pass out, get on all fours again—this time, lay on the ground with your knees lifted above the rest of your body. Move them back and forth slowly until they start to feel loose.

STEP NINE: Stretch out.

Stretching is the last thing you should do after working out because it's what allows your muscles to relax and get back to normal—and it feels fantastic! Stand with your arms stretched out above your head and squeeze them as hard as you can, then pull your arms forward even more until they are extended to their full length.

STEP TEN: Get a massage.

If you're looking for something a little different, then try giving yourself a massage because it lets your muscles relax even more and gives you a little pick-me-up in the process! Grab some lotion or Epson saltwater, and rub the areas where you've been working out until they feel great again.

STEP ELEVEN: Hydrate.

Water is essential to keep your muscles and the blood flowing throughout your body, so make sure you're staying hydrated during your workout! Be sure to drink a full cup of water for each pound of muscle you work out with (and if you don't have a scale, try using a measuring tape).

STEP TWELVE: Stretch some more.

Even though you've been working out, it's still often a good idea to stretch again after you finish exercising just in case something hurts. For this one, lie on the ground with both of your legs extended straight out in front of yourself and pull them up toward your body slowly until they feel great again.

I hope this helps you guys out! It might sound like a pain in the butt at first, but it really will save you money and make your life much easier in the long run. Have fun, and be sure to let me know how it goes when you finish your workout routine! :D
Posted by Faraz Mansouri at 16:51

Hi, I'm new to this site, but I have recently been hit by a box truck while working on a job. Now my legs are wobbly, and I feel tingles/burns in my thighs. Will this go away? Any advice will be appreciated. Thank you for your time :) Reply Delete

I'm sorry for your accident. Do you want to know if this injury has any treatments? Yes, please ask me more questions on this matter. I will be glad to answer. As a result, you may get some information about the treatments, including recovery time too. And don't worry about payment. As a patient-centric service provider, I will work with our medical experts to offer the best treatment within your budget. You can get more details about this if you ask me. I am always here to help and support your recovery. Please contact me directly through the following ways or write to my email address provided below as well. Thank you and have a nice day!! Email: support@medical-hospital-rehabilitation.org Reply Delete

Hello there, thank you for stopping by my site. I am Bekah, and I am a huge fan of your writing. I was thinking about how much time you must have put into this article. I have bookmarked it and saved it to my favorites. I enjoy reading your articles so much that I wonder if you could write an essay (or two) about where you are getting your information from? Simply curious. Thank you for sharing such excellent work with us here on this blog site!

# Conclusion

Most people have heard something about the importance of diet and exercise when it comes to longevity. But I'm sure you're wondering how much exercise you should do and what type of diet is best.

The link between diet and exercise is a significant one, so we'll start there... Age-related muscle loss can be slowed or halted by maintaining a high level of physical activity or training.

This makes sense for several reasons: muscle tissue burns more calories than fat tissue, so if you're healthier - on the cellular level - it makes sense you'll age better than someone who isn't as healthy.

You see, your muscles are a lot like your fat tissue - they can burn off energy through a process called thermogenesis. The mitochondria in muscle tissue can absorb glucose and fatty acids and use them as fuel. It's been shown that exercise improves mitochondrial energy production.

A recent study showed that when a compound found in green tea was combined with exercise, it boosted glutathione levels in mice's bodies more than exercising alone. Glutathione is our body's most potent antioxidant, and this antioxidant is depleted by exercise.

The bottom line is high levels of physical activity result in increased thermogenesis, energy production, reduced oxidative stress, and improved immune function. As if that wasn't enough, it's also been found that exercise helps optimize your hormones and cuts the risk of cancer.
The most effective way to remain healthy is by getting regular aerobic exercise and weight training.

The type of exercise you choose is not as critical, but it is essential to get plenty of aerobic activity. It's been shown that walking at a leisurely pace every day can add over six years to your life (7). So consider committing to daily walking if you need help forming a regular workout routine.

Why is walking so good for you? This type of exercise has been found to decrease stress levels while boosting your mood and immune system.

When you exercise at a moderate level for 45 minutes, your body releases several brain chemicals that make you feel good. The best news is that these chemicals don't need to be injected to affect your body. You can get the same benefits by simply walking every day.

It's recommended that adults get at least 30 minutes of moderate physical activity on most days (9). We've all heard the benefits of aerobic training: it boosts overall fitness, increases stamina, improves blood pressure, and increases bone density with each passing year. This type of exercise also enhances your immune system and helps keep the weight off.

To get the best cardiovascular workout, try to do some aerobic activity for at least 20 minutes. It's been shown that exercising in short bursts (such as 10 minutes of interval training) results in better cardiovascular fitness than doing a steady-state workout. Not only will you get more out of your training, but you'll also have more energy throughout the day.

If you aren't used to exercising or if you've become inactive, start slow. Work your way up to 30 minutes of aerobic exercise. Some people find that taking a brisk walk for about 20 minutes a day is enough to keep them feeling fit and healthy. Others prefer more prolonged bouts of exercise such as swimming laps or cycling for 45 minutes.

Once you've reached the 20-minute mark, decide whether or not you'd like to increase your workout. To get optimal results, be sure you're exercising at an intensity that makes it difficult to carry on a conversation. This will ensure that your training is practical.

Remember that women might want to train more than men due to age-related muscle loss and other concerns. If you're over 40 years old and haven't exercised in about ten years, begin with a slower exercise (like walking) before moving up to higher intensities. A beginner should start by exercising at about 75% of their maximum capacity. It's essential to avoid injury and ensure your body has time to adjust to the training.

After you've been exercising for a few weeks, you can measure your heart rate at rest and during exercise. Ideally, working out at an intensity of 80% or more of your maximum heart rate will give you the best cardiovascular benefits. You can use a calculator like this to help determine your heart rate at different intensities.

Weight training is also a great way to stay healthy and fit. According to some studies, weight training can improve muscle strength and aerobic capacity even in older adults. It can also help prevent age-related muscle loss, decrease your risk of injury and improve your body's ability to move.

The key is to make weight training a regular part of your fitness routine. A recent study showed that weight training for 24 weeks could increase their strength by about 30% (19). Another investigated the effects of three different exercise programs on older adults with type 2 diabetes mellitus. The results showed that all three exercise programs improved cardio-respiratory fitness and insulin sensitivity.

Studies also show that weight training can help senior citizens become more active, improving blood pressure and glucose levels. Since it works for your major muscle groups, set a goal to work out at least three times per week. You can also check out these muscle-building workouts for seniors for some ideas.

www.ingramcontent.com/pod-product-compliance
Lightning Source LLC
Chambersburg PA
CBHW071527080526
44588CB00011B/1577